Learn to Read

Activity Book

101 Fun Lessons to Teach Your Child to Read

HANNAH BRAUN, M. ED.

ZEPHYROS
PRESS

Learn to Read Activity Book

CONTENTS

INTRODUCTION **viii**

FOR PARENTS AND TEACHERS **ix**

The Lessons 1

1   Letter A **2**

2   Letter M **4**

3   Letter T **6**

4   Letter S **8**

5   Review **10**

6   Letter I **12**

7   Letter F **14**

8   Letter D **16**

9   Letter R **18**

10   Blending Known Letters **20**

11   Letter O **22**

12   Letter G **24**

13   Letter L **26**

14   Letter H **28**

15   Blending Known Letters **30**

16   The -at Word Family **32**

17   Letter U **34**

18   Letter C **36**

19   Letter B **38**

20   Letter N **40**

21   Blending Known Letters **42**

22   The -ot Word Family **44**

23   Letter K **46**

24   Letter V **48**

25   Letter E **50**

26   Letter W **52**

27   Blending Known Letters **54**

28   The -et Word Family **56**

29   Letter J **58**

30   Letter P **60**

31   Letter Y **62**

32   Letter X **64**

33   Blending Known Letters **66**

34   The -it Word Family **68**

35   Letter Q **70**

36   Letter Z **72**

37   The -an Word Family **74**

38   The -en Word Family **76**

39   The -in Word Family **78**

40   Review the Word Families -an,
     -en, and -in **80**

41   Sight Words *I* and *a* **82**

42   Sight Word *am* **84**

43   The -ip Word Family **86**

44   The -ug Word Family **88**

45   The -ap Word Family **90**

46   Review the Word Families -ip,
     -ug, and -ap **92**

47   Sight Word *have* **94**

48   Sight Word *we* **96**

49   The bl Blend **98**

50   The cl Blend **100**

51   The fl Blend **102**

52   Review the Blends bl, cl,
     and fl **104**

53   Sight Word *the* **106**

54   Sight Word *is* **108**

55   The gl Blend **110**

56   The pl Blend **112**

57   The sl Blend **114**

58   Review the Blends gl, pl,
     and sl **116**

59   Sight Word *are* **118**

60   Sight Word *you* **120**

61   The -id Word Family **122**

62   The -op Word Family **124**

63   The -ad Word Family **126**

64   Review the Word Families -id,
     -op, and -ad **128**

65   Sight Word *and* **130**

66   Sight Word *it* **132**

67   The br Blend **134**

68   The cr Blend **136**

69   The dr Blend **138**

70   Review the Blends br, cr,
     and dr **140**

71 The fr Blend **142**

72 The gr Blend **144**

73 The pr Blend **146**

74 The tr Blend **148**

75 Review the Blends fr, gr, pr, and tr **150**

76 Sight Word *in* **152**

77 Sight Word *was* **154**

78 The sm Blend **156**

79 The sc Blend **158**

80 The st Blend **160**

81 Review the Blends sm, sc, and st **162**

82 The /ch/ Sound **164**

83 Reading Words with the /ch/ Sound **166**

84 The /th/ Sound **168**

85 Reading Words with the /th/ Sound **170**

86 The /sh/ Sound **172**

87 Reading Words with the /sh/ Sound **174**

88 Review the Sounds /ch/, /th/, and /sh/ **176**

89 The -ash Word Family **178**

90 The -ush Word Family **180**

91 The -all Word Family **182**

92 The -ell Word Family **184**

93 The -ill Word Family **186**

94 Review the Word Families -all, -ell, and -ill **188**

95 The /ck/ Sound **190**

96 Reading Words with the /ck/ Sound **192**

97 The -ack Word Family **194**

98 The -ick Word Family **196**

99 The -ock Word Family **198**

100 Sight Word *this* **200**

101 Sight Word *for* **202**

RESOURCES **204**

INTRODUCTION

"He's probably saying, 'Arrrr! This be a heavy chest o' treasure!'" I say, in the most pirate-y voice I can muster. Satisfied, my son sits back in my lap, ready for the next page. Story time isn't complete for him without some ad-libbed dialogue between the characters. I relish this bedtime ritual where I pass on my love for reading. My son doesn't know that these early literacy experiences are laying the foundation for his eventual independent reading of textbooks, emails, and comics. Parents and teachers are in a unique position to guide children down the path to literacy. It's both a responsibility and an honor.

When you guide a child toward a new skill, like cooking, shooting a basketball, or tying a shoe, you stand side by side with them through challenges and successes. It's something to bond over. Teaching a child to read is similar. As you work through the lessons and games that follow, you are passing down a skill that will powerfully impact the child's life. It will bring them enjoyment and independence for years to come.

To write this book, I drew on my undergraduate and graduate studies in the field of education as well as the eight years I spent in the classroom refining my craft with a diverse group of students. But the most helpful thing, I've found, is simply to observe and participate as my own two children gain language and literacy. My greatest reward as both a teacher and a mom is to witness the "lightbulb" moments when kids grasp a new skill, gain confidence, and blossom right before my eyes.

I wrote this book as a tool to help you take on the important task of teaching a child to read. I am confident that you can bring about "lightbulb" moments for your child or student as you bond over reading.

FOR PARENTS AND TEACHERS

How to Use This Book

The lessons in this book are designed around a research-based teaching model called explicit instruction. Explicit instruction lessons start with a review of previously learned material, followed by a clear statement of the lesson's objective. You'll see a simple sentence that lets the child know exactly what they will be focusing on in the lesson. Next, the lesson follows an "I do, we do, you do" format:

I DO The "I do" portion involves the adult modeling the target skill. It might consist of demonstrating a letter sound or blending a phonics pattern. Think about how you learned to change a tire or fry an egg—you probably watched someone else who was proficient in that skill do it first. Here, you are the proficient reader giving the child a glimpse into how your brain does the work of reading.

WE DO The "we do" portion of the lesson is for guided practice. Think of it as training wheels on a bike. The child takes on some responsibility for trying the skill, and the adult gives corrective guidance or feedback. The child might be asked to make the shape of a letter or say each sound in a word. If the child makes a mistake, gently offer a correction and maybe even model the skill again. Guided practice should continue until the child is able to perform the skill correctly.

YOU DO In the "you do" portion of the lesson, the child practices independently. This allows the child to develop automaticity with the skill. The games and activities in this book are designed for independent practice. Of course, it can be both beneficial and fun for the adult to join in, too! Just make sure it's the child who is doing the mental "heavy lifting" during this time.

The book starts by introducing one letter at a time. I chose this particular sequence of letters so that children can quickly start to blend together simple words even before they know the whole alphabet. It's exciting for children to get the payoff of reading an actual word, like *am*, after just two lessons rather than working for weeks learning letters but not actually getting to read. Sight word and word family lessons are also found throughout the book.

Before teaching a lesson, you may want to read through it on your own to familiarize yourself with the content. Your starting point within the book and your pace will depend on the child. If the child is new to learning letters, you may need to introduce one letter and then practice identifying it in other texts and making its sound for a few days before moving on to the next lesson. Other children with some familiarity with letters may move through more than one lesson in a sitting.

Be sensitive to the cues the child is showing you. If they are getting antsy or frustrated, they may need a break or the lesson may be too hard. Every child learns at a different pace. It's okay to repeat a lesson or skip ahead.

Setting Expectations

There are many possible paths and paces for completing this book. Ideally, you want to work with a child in their "zone of proximal development"—the point just a little beyond what they can do on their own. The child is the one who will dictate this level and pace. As a benchmark, some preschool and kindergarten classes focus on one letter per week. By first grade, children will probably review a few letters a week and then move on to other skills.

When working on lessons, keep in mind that young children have a short attention span. Most kindergarten teachers don't spend more than 20 minutes on an activity because by then, children mentally and physically need to move on. If you notice the child getting restless before you have made it through the lesson and game, take a break and come back later.

Use the following indicators to determine whether the child needs a faster or slower pace:

PRIOR LITERACY EXPERIENCES How much has the child been read to? Do they recognize symbols, such as restaurant logos? Do they point to letters in their environment and identify them? Do they pretend to read text that they see? If the child shows no interest in text, it is best to save this book for later and build them up with other literacy experiences, like reading picture books, pointing out words on food packaging, and identifying frequently seen symbols. If the child has been read to and is beginning to point to text and guess or ask what it says, they may be ready to work through the lessons at a slow pace. If the child can already identify some letters, they may be able to move through the lessons at a quick pace.

ABILITY TO IMITATE After you model the skill in a lesson, watch the child closely. Are they able to imitate what you showed them after a few tries? If not, they may need to go back to a previous lesson. It's also possible that the child may not be developmentally ready to do what you are asking. If so, take a break from the book and enjoy reading to them. Try again in a couple of months. If the child flies through the guided practice and the game, you may be able to skip ahead.

CONCEPT RETENTION When you review the previous lesson, does the child seem to remember what they learned? If they cannot remember at all, they probably need a slower pace. If they remember right away or with a little prompting, your pace is probably good.

Our current culture seems to place a lot of emphasis on children meeting standards and benchmarks by a certain time. Keep in mind that all children progress differently, and trying to force a child to do something they are not developmentally ready for will only cause frustration for everyone involved. It's important to preserve within the child a positive attitude toward reading, and you can do this by following their pace.

Motivating Kids

Learning to read is hard work, and it's important to help kids stay motivated in the process. Here are some ways to encourage motivation:

PRAISE EFFORT As children learn, they make approximations of the skills we demonstrate for them. Sometimes they are successful right away, which is motivating in itself. Other times they aren't totally accurate until after several tries. This can get discouraging. Provide verbal praise when your child demonstrates effort, even if their performance isn't completely correct. If possible, point out specific behaviors the child is demonstrating that show you they are on the right path. This will encourage them to repeat those behaviors. Then, gently guide them toward accuracy, like in these examples:

> *I love how you pointed to each word in the sentence as you read so that you wouldn't leave any out. Let's go back and double-check what the second word says.*

> *Wow! You read the first sound in that word perfectly. Great job! Listen to how I blend the ending, and then try it again.*

OFFER CHOICE The provided lessons suggest ways to practice letter sounds, shapes, and phonics patterns. However, you and the child may have other ideas and preferences. Choice is a powerful motivator—especially for children, who don't often have much power. Providing choice through the lessons might sound like this:

> *I can see that you're tired of tracing the letters on the page. Would you like to try writing them a different way? Maybe you'd like to use a whiteboard or make the letters with clay.*

> *Would you like to practice finding letter T in this game, or would you rather look for letter T in one of your picture books?*

> *Let's try something silly. Can you read these words in a different voice? Would you like to read in a robot voice or an opera singer voice? Maybe you can think of a different voice to try.*

CONSIDER INCREMENTAL REWARDS Many children respond well to working toward a reward. This could be a small food treat or a sticker for completing a lesson. The child could earn extra screen time or the chance to pick from a treasure box. If the child can handle more delayed gratification, you could offer a bigger reward for completing a few lessons. For instance, five completed lessons could be rewarded with a trip to a special park or the ice cream shop.

Out and About

Your reading instruction will be most effective if you find other ways, beyond this book, to reinforce literacy concepts. Here are a few ideas:

- Encourage the child to identify letters and words on signs, packaging, logos, and so on.
- Play an "I spy" game: *I spy something that starts with letter B.* Then the child tries to guess what it is. Trade roles.
- Read alphabet books to give the child more exposure to letter sounds.
- Send your child on "missions": *Can you find me something in this room that rhymes with bug? Can you touch two things that start with the letter L?* Games like this are perfect when you have a few minutes to fill.
- Make letters or words out of unconventional materials: Arrange sugar packets at a restaurant into letters. Draw letters in shaving cream on the wall of the tub. Make letters by lining up toy cars or dry pasta.
- Expose the child to toys with letters. Alphabet puzzles, magnetic letters, or electronic toys that make letter sounds are all helpful.
- Check out books from the easy-reader section of the library. At first you will need to read the books to the child, but they will gradually start to recognize more and more of the words on their own.

The Lessons

Letter A

1. Share the objective.

Say: *Today we'll learn what letter A looks like and sounds like. Learning letter sounds will help you read words.*

2. Teach the letter shape.

Point to the letters. Say: *This is letter A. There is a big A and a little A. Watch how I trace the letters with my finger. Can you trace the letters with your finger?*

3. Teach the letter sound.

Say: *The letter A makes the sound /a/, like at the beginning of alligator. Can you open and close your arms like an alligator's mouth chomping? Let's make the A sound while you make your arms chomp like an alligator: /a/ /a/ alligator.*

Repeat after me: /a/ /a/ apple, /a/ /a/ ant, /a/ /a/ ax.

4. Practice blending skills.

Say: *Let's play a listening game. I'll say two sounds and I want you to put them together to make a word. If I say /an/ /t/, you say "ant."*

/app/ /le/, /an/ /d/, /af/ /ter/

> When children know what they will be learning and how it will help them, they are more likely to pay attention to the lesson.

> When a letter is shown between slashes, say the letter's sound, not its name.

The Ant Goes Marching

Color the boxes with the letter A to make a path for the ant to get to the food.

🐜	y	a	a	a	r
a	t	a	m	a	a
a	a	a	x	w	🌭

Circle the Picture

Say the name of each picture. Circle the pictures that begin with the /a/ sound.

Letter M

1. Review.

Look back at the letter A in the previous lesson. Practice /a/ /a/ alligator with the arm-chomping motion.

2. Share the objective.

Say: *Today we'll learn what letter M looks like and sounds like.*

3. Teach the letter shape.

Point to the letters. Say: *This is letter M. There is a big M and a little M. Watch how I trace the letters with my finger, then you try.*

4. Teach the letter sound.

Say: *The letter M makes the sound /m/, like at the beginning of monkey. Let's make the M sound while you swing your arms like a monkey: /m/ /m/ monkey.*

Repeat after me: /m/ /m/ marker, /m/ /m/ mask, /m/ /m/ milk.

> Say the M sound with a closed mouth ("mmm"). Avoid adding a vowel sound at the end ("muh").

5. Practice blending skills.

Say: *I'll say two sounds and I want you to put them together to make a word. If I say /mo/ /p/, you say "mop."*

/mil/ /k/, /ma/ /n/, /mo/ /m/

> Being able to identify and manipulate sounds in words is called phonemic awareness and is an important building block in learning to read.

Moon and Stars

Color each star with the letter M.

M in the Middle

Draw a line from each picture that starts with M to the letters in the middle.

Mm

Letter T

1. Review.

Look back at the letter M in the previous lesson. Practice /m/ /m/ monkey with the swinging-arms motion.

> Review letter A, as well, if the child has the attention span for it.

2. Share the objective.

Say: *Today we'll learn what letter T looks like and sounds like.*

3. Teach the letter shape.

Point to the letters. Say: *This is letter T. There is a big T and a little T. Can you trace the two letters with your finger?*

4. Teach the letter sound.

Say: *The letter T makes the sound /t/, like at the beginning of tiger. Let's make the T sound while you make tiger claws: /t/ /t/ tiger.*

Repeat after me: /t/ /t/ turtle, /t/ /t/ teeth, /t/ /t/ truck.

> Say the T sound in a very short way. Avoid adding a vowel sound at the end ("tuh").

5. Practice blending skills.

Say: *I'll say two sounds and I want you to put them together to make a word. If I say /tai/ /l/, you say "tail."*

/ta/ /p/, /te/ /ll/, /too/ /k/

Tricky Tiger

Circle each letter T.

Shop Till You Drop

Circle the things you could buy that start with T.

Letter S

1. Review.

Look back at the letter T in the previous lesson. Practice /t/ /t/ tiger with the tiger claw motion.

2. Share the objective.

Say: *Today we'll learn what letter S looks like and sounds like.*

3. Teach the letter shape.

Point to the letters. Say: *This is letter S. There is a big S and a little S. Can you trace the two letters with your finger?*

4. Teach the letter sound.

Say: *The letter S makes the sound /s/, like at the beginning of snake. Let's make the S sound while you move like a snake: /s/ /s/ snake.*

Repeat after me: /s/ /s/ sock, /s/ /s/ sun, /s/ /s/ snail.

> The S sound should be made with the teeth together ("sss"). Avoid adding a vowel sound at the end ("suh").

5. Practice blending skills.

Say: *I'll say two sounds and I want you to put them together to make a word. If I say /sto/ /p/, you say "stop."*

/sli/ /ck/, /soa/ /p/, /sof/ /t/

Snake through the Maze

Connect each letter S to get through the maze.

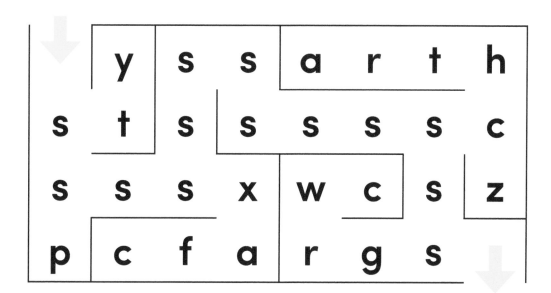

	y	s	s	a	r	t	h
s	t	s	s	s	s	s	c
s	s	s	x	w	c	s	z
p	c	f	a	r	g	s	

Snacks for the Snake

The snake wants to eat only things that start with S. Draw a line from each food that starts with S to a letter S.

S   S   S

Review

1. Review letter sounds.

Point to the letters and say: *Can you remember the sound and shape for each of these letters?*

2. Demonstrate finding beginning sounds.

Say: *Listen carefully to the beginning of this word: tail. It has a T sound at the beginning: /t/ /t/ tail.*

Listen for the beginning sound again: mask. It has an M sound at the beginning: /m/ /m/ mask.

3. Practice finding beginning sounds.

Say: *Now you try to find the letter that matches the beginning sound. It will be one of the four letters shown: soft, ask, tire, mind.*

> Allow some quiet thinking time after each word. Encourage the child to say the word on their own to find the beginning sound.

Uppercase and Lowercase Match

Draw lines to connect each uppercase letter with the matching lowercase letter.

A M T S

m s a t

Which Is Right?

Circle the letter that you hear at the beginning of each picture.

t a   s m   m a

s a   t s   m t

Letter I

1. Share the objective.

Say: *Today we'll learn what letter I looks like and sounds like.*

2. Teach the letter shape.

Point to the letters. Say: *This is letter I. There is a big I and a little I. Can you use your whole body to make an I shape?*

> Movements and gestures help children remember new things.

3. Teach the letter sound.

Say: *The letter I makes the sound /i/, like at the beginning of igloo. Can you curve your arms over your head to make it look like you're in an igloo? Let's make the I sound while you pretend to be in an igloo: /i/ /i/ igloo.*

Repeat after me: /i/ /i/ inchworm, /i/ /i/ insect, /i/ /i/ iguana.

4. Practice blending skills.

Say: *I'll say two sounds and I want you to put them together to make a word: /in/ /side/, /in/ /sect/, /in/ /fant/.*

Inchworm Adventure

Color the boxes with the letter I to make a path for the inchworm to get to the leaf.

🐛	i	x	b	t	s
v	i	i	i	i	i
a	a	a	x	w	🍃

Picture Perfect

Imagine that you are taking pictures of only things that start with I. Draw a line from each item that starts with I to the letters in the middle.

Letter F

1. Review.

Look back at the letter I in the previous lesson. Practice
/i/ /i/ igloo with arms shaped like an igloo.

2. Share the objective.

Say: *Today we'll learn what letter F looks like and sounds like.*

3. Teach the letter shape.

Point to the letters. Say: *This is letter F. There is a big F and a
little F. Can you use your whole body to make an F shape?*

4. Teach the letter sound.

Say: *The letter F makes the sound /f/, like at the beginning of
fish. Let's make the F sound while you swim like a fish: /f/ /f/ fish.
Repeat after me: /f/ /f/ flag, /f/ /f/ fan, /f/ /f/ frog.*

> The F sound should
> be airy and sound like
> "fff." Avoid adding a
> vowel sound at the
> end ("fuh").

5. Practice blending skills.

Say: *I'll say two sounds and I want you to put them together to
make a word: /f/ /lip/, /f/ /ox/, /f/ /ind/.*

Leaping Lily Pads

Color each lily pad with the letter F.

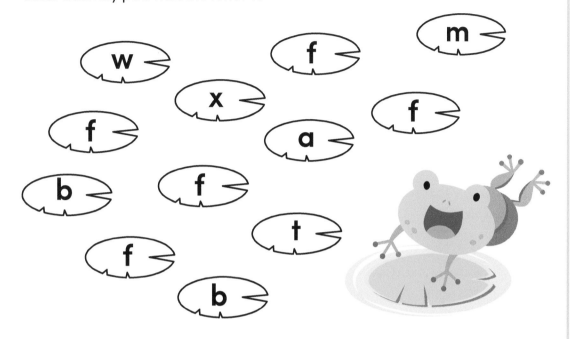

Spin and Go

Choose something to mark your place, like a piece of cereal. Use the tip of a pencil to hold a paper clip loop to the center of the spinner. Flick the paper clip. If it lands on something that starts with F, move two spaces. If it lands on something that doesn't start with F, move one space.

Letter D

1. Review.

Look back at the letter F in the previous lesson. Practice /f/ /f/ fish with the swimming motion.

2. Share the objective.

Say: *Today we'll learn what letter D looks like and sounds like.*

3. Teach the letter shape.

Point to the letters. Say: *This is letter D. There is a big D and a little D. Can you write the letters in the air with a pretend magic wand?*

4. Teach the letter sound.

Say: *The letter D makes the sound /d/, like at the beginning of duck. Can you flap your elbows like a duck's wings? Let's make the D sound while you move like a duck: /d/ /d/ duck.*

Repeat after me: /d/ /d/ dog, /d/ /d/ door, /d/ /d/ dinosaur.

5. Practice blending skills.

Say: *I'll say two sounds and I want you to put them together to make a word: /d/ /ish/, /d/ /ive/, /d/ /ent/.*

Letter D Duck Hunt

Circle each letter D.

Circle the Picture

Say the name of each picture. Circle the pictures that begin with D.

Letter R

1. Review.

Look back at the letter D in the previous lesson. Practice /d/ /d/ duck with the elbow-flapping motion.

2. Share the objective.

Say: *Today we'll learn what letter R looks like and sounds like.*

3. Teach the letter shape.

Point to the letters. Say: *This is letter R. There is a big R and a little R. Can you draw the letters on the floor with your foot?*

4. Teach the letter sound.

Say: *The letter R makes the sound /r/, like at the beginning of rabbit. Let's make the R sound while you hop like a rabbit: /r/ /r/ rabbit.*

Repeat after me: /r/ /r/ race car, /r/ /r/ rainbow, /r/ /r/ ring.

> The R sound should be a continuous "rrr." Avoid adding a vowel sound at the end ("ruh").

5. Practice blending skills.

Say: *I'll say two sounds and I want you to put them together to make a word: /r/ /ide/, /r/ /aft/, /r/ /est/.*

Race through the Maze

Connect each letter R to get through the maze.

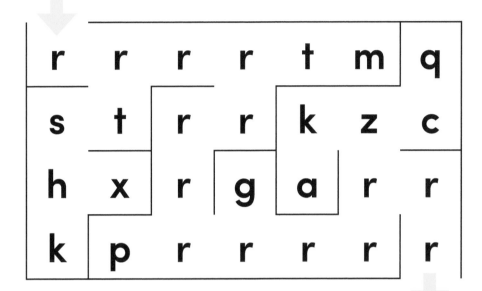

Rabbits 'Round the Garden

Each rabbit found something in the garden that starts with R.
Circle the thing each rabbit found.

Blending Known Letters

1. Review.

Say: *Can you remember the sound and shape for each of these letters?*

2. Share the objective.

Say: *Today you will learn how to blend sounds that you know to make words.*

3. Demonstrate blending sounds.

Say: *Watch how I put my finger on each dot and make the sound of the letter. Listen to how I slide through the sounds to make a word.*

Slowly run your finger across the arrow and say /aaammm/. Repeat this motion and sound a couple of times more quickly until you are saying the word *am* at a normal speed.

Repeat this process with the word *fit*.

4. Guide the practice.

Have the child point to each dot under the word *am* and say the individual letter sounds. Then have them move their finger across the arrow, sliding through all the sounds to make a word. Repeat with the word *fit*.

> If the child needs more support, try making the individual letter sounds and then blending the word with your voices together.

Blend and Match

Touch the dots and say each sound in the first word. Then slide through the sounds to blend them into a word. Draw a line to connect each word to the matching picture.

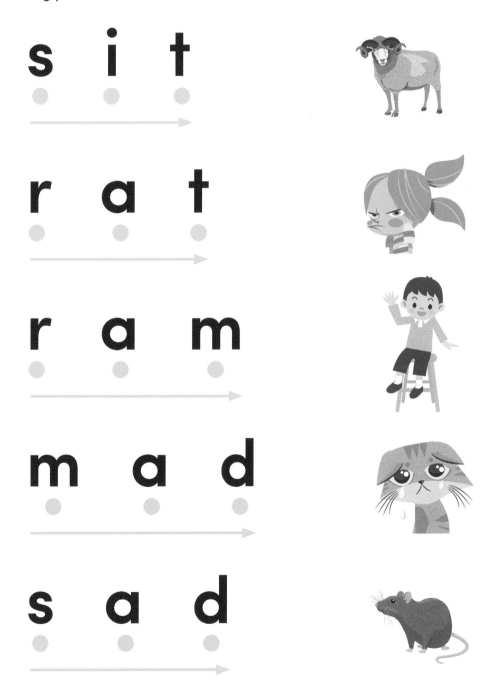

s i t

r a t

r a m

m a d

s a d

Letter O

1. Review.

Practice blending some words in the previous lesson.

2. Share the objective.

Say: *Today we'll learn what letter O looks like and sounds like.*

3. Teach the letter shape.

Point to the letters. Say: *This is letter O. There is a big O and a little O. Can you trace the two letters with your finger?*

4. Teach the letter sound.

Say: *The letter O makes the sound /o/, like at the beginning of octopus. Let's make the O sound while you move your arms like octopus tentacles: /o/ /o/ octopus.*

Repeat after me: /o/ /o/ ostrich, /o/ /o/ octagon, /o/ /o/ olive.

5. Practice sound discrimination skills.

Say: *Listen to the first sound of each word and tell me if it starts with /o/: otter, bike, off.*

Three in a Row

Draw lines to connect three letter Os in a row. The lines can be vertical, horizontal, or diagonal.

o l f q x e w

o t z i n v o

o m c a o o o

b o u k o d o

r g o o o j p

On to the Zoo!

Oliver wants to see lots of things that start with O at the zoo. Draw a line from each animal that starts with O to the letters in the center.

Oo

Letter G

1. Review.

Look back at the letter O in the previous lesson.
Practice /o/ /o/ octopus with the tentacle-arms motion.

2. Share the objective.

Say: *Today we'll learn what letter G looks like and sounds like.*

3. Teach the letter shape.

Point to the letters. Say: *This is letter G. There is a big G and a little G. Can you draw the shape of the letters in the air with your elbow?*

4. Teach the letter sound.

Say: *The letter G makes the sound /g/, like at the beginning of grasshopper. Let's make the G sound while you make your hand hop like a grasshopper: /g/ /g/ grasshopper.*

Repeat after me: /g/ /g/ grapes, /g/ /g/ glove, /g/ /g/ gate.

5. Practice blending skills.

Say: *I'll say three sounds and I want you to put them together to make a word: /g/ /a/ /p/, /g/ /o/ /t/, /g/ /u/ /m/.*

Color the Gumballs

Color each gumball with the letter G.

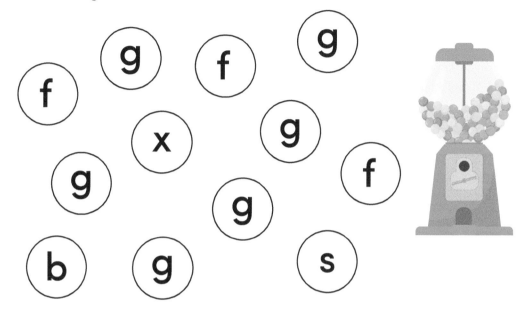

Find the Beginning Sound

Circle the letter that you hear at the beginning of each picture. Some pictures start with G. Some pictures start with other letters that you know.

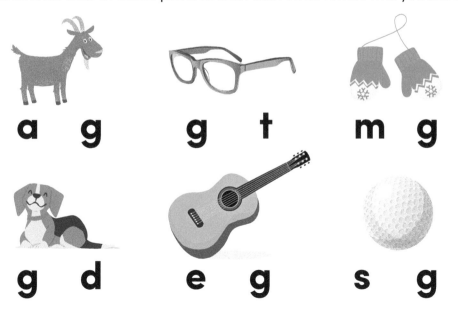

Letter L

1. Review.

Look back at the letter G in the previous lesson.

Practice /g/ /g/ grasshopper with the hopping-hand motion.

2. Share the objective.

Say: *Today we'll learn what letter L looks like and sounds like.*

3. Teach the letter shape.

Point to the letters. Say: *This is letter L. There is a big L and a little L. Can you make the shape of each L using your arms?*

4. Teach the letter sound.

Say: *The letter L makes the sound /l/, like at the beginning of lobster. Let's make the L sound while you make lobster claws: /l/ /l/ lobster.*

Repeat after me: /l/ /l/ lion, /l/ /l/ ladder, /l/ /l/ leaf.

> Make the L sound as a continuous "lll." Avoid adding a vowel sound at the end ("luh").

5. Practice sound discrimination skills.

Say: *Listen to the first sound of each word and tell me if it starts with /l/: mad, love, look.*

Lost Ladybug

Color the boxes with the letter L to make a path for the ladybug to get to the leaf.

🐞	l	x	b	t	s
v	l	l	l	l	l
a	a	a	x	w	🍃

Spin and Go

Choose something to mark your place, like a piece of cereal. Use the tip of a pencil to hold a paper clip loop to the center of the spinner. Flick the paper clip. If it lands on something that starts with L, move two spaces. If it lands on something that doesn't start with L, move one space.

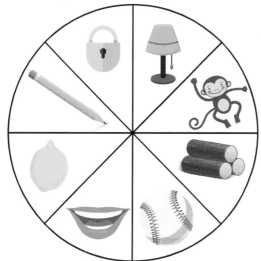

Letter H

1. Review.

Look back at the letter L in the previous lesson. Practice /l/ /l/ lobster with the lobster claw motion.

2. Share the objective.

Say: *Today we'll learn what letter H looks like and sounds like.*

3. Teach the letter shape.

Point to the letters. Say: *This is letter H. There is a big H and a little H. Can you trace the two letters with your finger?*

4. Teach the letter sound.

Say: *The letter H makes the sound /h/, like at the beginning of horse. Can you tap your hands on the table like a horse's hooves running? Let's make the H sound while you tap your hands: /h/ /h/ horse.*

Repeat after me: /h/ /h/ hat, /h/ /h/ house, /h/ /h/ hammer.

> The H sound should be a short puff of air, as if you were fogging up a mirror.

5. Practice blending skills.

Say: *I'll say three sounds and I want you to put them together to make a word: If I say /h/ /e/ /n/, you say "hen."*

/h/ /o/ /p/, /h/ /u/ /m/, /h/ /a/ /m/

Hunt for H

Circle each letter H.

Circle the Picture

Say the name of each picture. Circle the pictures that begin with H.

Blending Known Letters

1. Review.

Say: *Can you remember the sound and shape for each of these letters?*

2. Share the objective.

Say: *Today you will learn how to blend sounds that you know to make words.*

3. Demonstrate blending sounds.

Say: *Watch how I put my finger on each dot and make the sound of the letter. Listen to how I slide through the sounds to make a word.*

Slowly run your finger across the arrow and say /lllooog/. Repeat this motion and sound a couple of times more quickly until you are saying the word *log* at a normal speed.

Repeat this process with the word *hot*.

4. Guide the practice.

Have the child point to each dot under the word *log* and say the individual letter sounds. Then have them move their finger across the arrow, sliding through all the sounds to make a word. Repeat with the word *hot*.

Blend and Match

Touch the dots and say each sound in the first word. Then slide through the sounds to blend them into a word. Draw a line to connect each word to the matching picture.

d o g

h a t

l i d

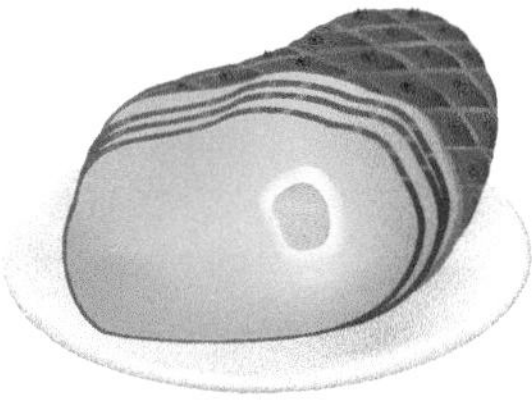

r a g

h a m

The -at Word Family

1. Review.

Say: *Can you remember the sounds for the letters A and T? Can you slide your finger across the arrow and blend the sounds together?*

2. Share the objective.

Say: *Today you will learn how to read words that end with /at/.*

3. Demonstrate reading new words with -at.

Say: *Watch how I can read more words by putting different sounds in front of /at/.*

Touch the dot under the S in *sat* and say /s/, then slide your finger across the short arrow and say /at/. Slide your finger across the long arrow and say "sat."

Have the child try blending *sat*. Repeat this process with *hat*.

4. Practice rhyming skills.

Say: *When two words have the same ending sound, they rhyme. Sat and hat rhyme because they both have the /at/ sound at the end. Listen to these two words and tell me if they rhyme: flat, cat. How about pat and mat? How about sat and run?*

> Practicing rhyming helps children read and spell by analogy. If they can read and spell *cat*, they can use this knowledge to read and spell other words that end with the /at/ sound.

Word Family Fun

Color each circle that has a word or a picture from the -at family.

Letter U

1. Review.

Practice reading the -at family words in the previous lesson.

2. Share the objective.

Say: *Today we'll learn what letter U looks like and sounds like.*

3. Teach the letter shape.

Point to the letters. Say: *This is letter U. There is a big U and a little U. Can you use your arms to make the letter U?*

4. Teach the letter sound.

Say: *The letter U makes the sound /u/, like at the beginning of up. Let's make the U sound while you point your fingers up to the ceiling: /u/ /u/ up.*

Repeat after me: /u/ /u/ upset, /u/ /u/ under, /u/ /u/ ugly.

5. Practice blending skills.

Say: *I'll say three sounds and I want you to put them together to make a word: /g/ /u/ /m/, /c/ /u/ /t/, /t/ /u/ /g/.*

Three in a Row

Draw lines to connect three letter Us in a row. The lines can be vertical, horizontal, or diagonal.

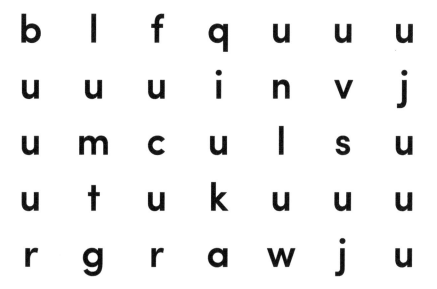

b   l   f   q   u   u   u

u   u   u   i   n   v   j

u   m   c   u   l   s   u

u   t   u   k   u   u   u

r   g   r   a   w   j   u

What Begins with U?

Draw a line from each picture that starts with U to a letter U.

u   u   u   u

Letter C

1. Review.

Look back at the letter U in the previous lesson.
Practice /u/ /u/ up while pointing up to the ceiling.

2. Share the objective.

Say: *Today we'll learn what letter C looks like and sounds like.*

3. Teach the letter shape.

Point to the letters. Say: *This is letter C. There is a big C and a little C. Can you make a letter C with your hand?*

4. Teach the letter sound.

Say: *The letter C makes the sound /c/, like at the beginning of car. Let's make the C sound while you pretend to drive a car: /c/ /c/ car.*

Repeat after me: /c/ /c/ cat, /c/ /c/ cow, /c/ /c/ cactus.

> The C sound should be a short, hard sound coming from the back of the tongue touching the roof of the mouth. Avoid adding a vowel sound at the end ("cuh").

5. Practice sound discrimination skills.

Say: *Listen to the first sound of each word and tell me if it starts with /c/: curl, trip, clue.*

Connect the Cs

Connect the letter Cs to get through the maze.

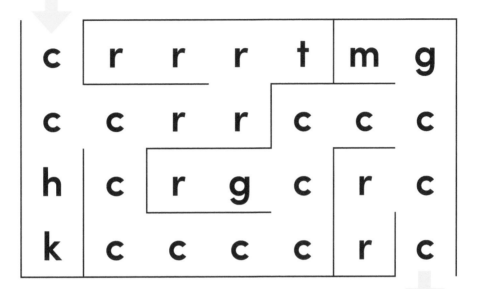

c	r	r	r	t	m	g
c	c	r	r	c	c	c
h	c	r	g	c	r	c
k	c	c	c	c	r	c

Tasty Treats

Each child chose a special treat that starts with C. Circle the treat that each child chose.

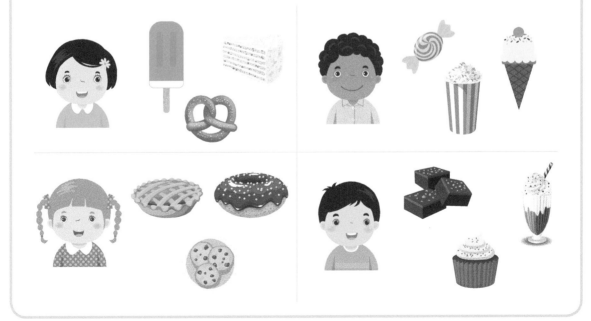

Letter B

1. Review.

Look back at the letter C in the previous lesson. Practice
/c/ /c/ car while doing the driving motion.

2. Share the objective.

Say: *Today we'll learn what letter B looks like and sounds like.*

3. Teach the letter shape.

Point to the letters. Say: *This is letter B. There is a big B and
a little B. Can you trace the two letters with your finger?*

4. Teach the letter sound.

Say: *The letter B makes the sound /b/, like at the beginning
of bat. Let's make the B sound while you flap your arms like
a bat's wings: /b/ /b/ bat.*

Repeat after me: /b/ /b/ bear, /b/ /b/ ball, /b/ /b/ balloon.

5. Practice blending skills.

Say: *I'll say three sounds and I want you to put them together to
make a word: /b/ /a/ /d/, /b/ /e/ /d/, /b/ /i/ /t/.*

Batter Up!

Color each ball with the letter B.

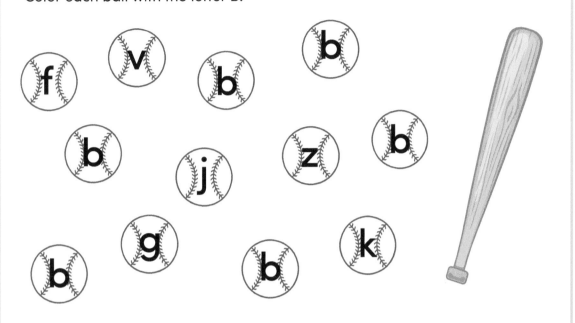

Bianca's Bedroom

Bianca has many things in her room that start with B. Draw a line from each item that starts with B to the letters in the center.

Letter N

1. Review.

Look back at the letter B in the previous lesson. Practice /b/ /b/ bat with the arm-flapping motion.

2. Share the objective.

Say: *Today we'll learn what letter N looks like and sounds like.*

3. Teach the letter shape.

Point to the letters. Say: *This is letter N. There is a big N and a little N. Can you write the letters in the air with a pretend magic wand?*

4. Teach the letter sound.

Say: *The letter N makes the sound /n/, like at the beginning of nose. Let's make the N sound while you tap your nose: /n/ /n/ nose.*

Repeat after me: /n/ /n/ nest, /n/ /n/ nail, /n/ /n/ necklace.

5. Practice identifying beginning sounds.

Say: *Listen closely and tell me the beginning sound in each word: nap, cam, not.*

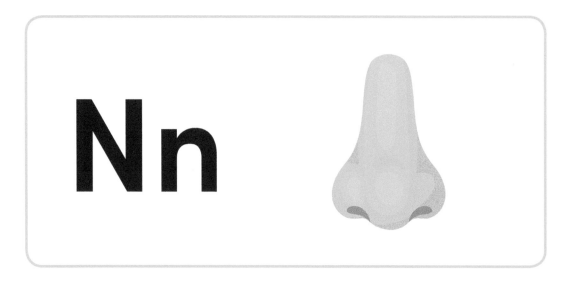

Near the Nest

Circle each letter N.

Spin and Go

Choose something to mark your place, like a piece of cereal. Use the tip of a pencil to hold a paper clip loop to the center of the spinner. Flick the paper clip. If it lands on something that starts with N, move two spaces. If it lands on something that doesn't start with N, move one space.

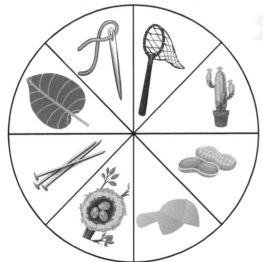

Blending Known Letters

1. Review.

Say: *Can you remember the sound and shape for each of these letters?*

2. Share the objective.

Say: *Today you will learn how to blend sounds that you know to make words.*

3. Demonstrate blending sounds.

Say: *Watch how I put my finger on each dot and make the sound of the letter. Listen to how I slide through the sounds to make a word.*

Slowly run your finger across the arrow and say /cuuub/. Repeat this motion and sound a couple of times more quickly until you are saying the word *cub* at a normal speed.

Repeat this process with the word *can*.

4. Guide the practice.

Have the child point to each dot under the word *cub* and say the individual letter sounds. Then have them move their finger across the arrow, sliding through all the sounds to make a word. Repeat with the word *can*.

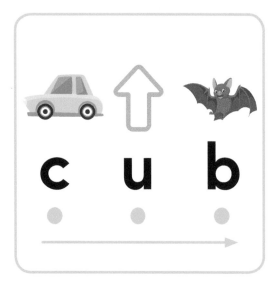

Slide Through and Circle

Say each letter sound. Blend the sounds together to make a word. Circle the picture that matches the word.

r a n

s u n

c a t

t a g

h o g

The -ot Word Family

1. Review.

Say: *Can you remember the sounds for the letters O and T? Can you slide your finger across the arrow and blend the sounds together?*

2. Share the objective.

Say: *Today you will learn how to read words that end with /ot/.*

3. Demonstrate reading new words with -ot.

Say: *Watch how I can read more words by putting different sounds in front of /ot/.*

Touch the dot under the D in *dot* and say /d/, then slide your finger across the short arrow and say /ot/. Slide your finger across the long arrow and say "dot."

Have the child try blending *dot*. Repeat this process with *lot*.

4. Practice rhyming skills.

Say: *I will say two words and I want you to tell me if they rhyme: spot, fan. How about lot and rot? How about cot and not?*

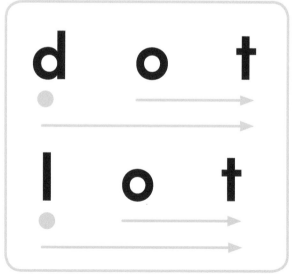

Help Bot

Color the boxes with words from the -ot family to make a path for the robot to get to its house. Read the -ot words.

	not	lot	got
am	I	him	dot
ram		hot	tot
can	sit	cot	gal
	ham	rot	

Letter K

1. Review.

Practice reading the -ot family words in the previous lesson.

2. Share the objective.

Say: *Today we'll learn what letter K looks like and sounds like.*

3. Teach the letter shape.

Point to the letters. Say: *This is letter K. There is a big K and a little K. Can you trace the two letters with your finger?*

4. Teach the letter sound.

Say: *The letter K makes the sound /k/, like at the beginning of key. Let's make the K sound while you pretend to turn a key in a lock: /k/ /k/ key.*

Repeat after me: /k/ /k/ kite, /k/ /k/ kangaroo, /k/ /k/ king.

> The K sound is the same as the C sound, short and hard.

5. Practice blending skills.

Say: *I'll say three sounds and I want you to put them together to make a word: /k/ /ee/ /p/, /k/ /i/ /ck/, /k/ /i/ /ss/.*

Connect the Ks

Connect the letter Ks to get through the maze.

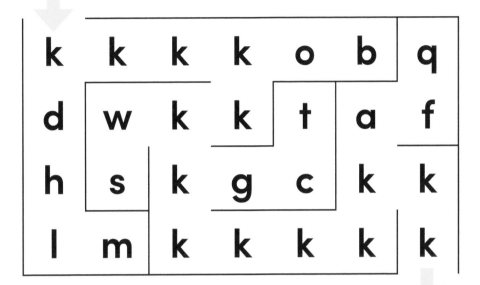

Circle the Picture

Say the name of each picture. Circle the pictures that begin with K.

Letter V

1. Review.

Look back at the letter K in the previous lesson. Practice /k/ /k/ key with the key-turning motion.

2. Share the objective.

Say: *Today we'll learn what letter V looks like and sounds like.*

3. Teach the letter shape.

Point to the letters. Say: *This is letter V. There is a big V and a little V. Can you use your body to make the letter V?*

4. Teach the letter sound.

Say: *The letter V makes the sound /v/, like at the beginning of violin. Let's make the V sound while you pretend to play a violin: /v/ /v/ violin.*

Repeat after me: /v/ /v/ vest, /v/ /v/ vegetables, /v/ /v/ vase.

> The V sound is a continuous "vvv." Avoid adding a vowel sound at the end ("vuh").

5. Practice identifying beginning sounds.

Say: *I'll say three words and I want you to tell me which one doesn't start with V: vote, vet, stop. Let's try again: vine, blue, very.*

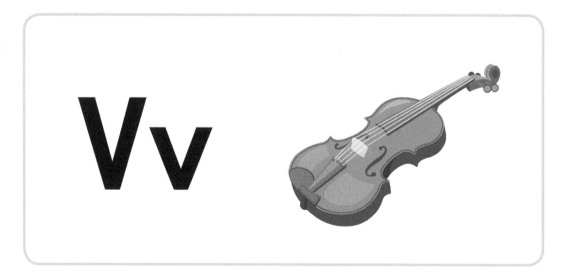

Three in a Row

Draw lines to connect three letter Vs in a row. The lines can be vertical, horizontal, or diagonal.

b l v v v r o

s w u i v m v

x m c j v s v

z d t v h u v

v v v a w j g

Connect to the Center

Draw a line from each item that starts with V to the letters in the center.

Vv

Letter E

1. Review.

Look back at the letter V in the previous lesson. Practice /v/ /v/ violin while pretending to play a violin.

2. Share the objective.

Say: *Today we'll learn what letter E looks like and sounds like.*

3. Teach the letter shape.

Point to the letters. Say: *This is letter E. There is a big E and a little E. Can you write the letters in the air with a pretend magic wand?*

4. Teach the letter sound.

Say: *The letter E makes the sound /e/, like at the beginning of elephant. Let's make the E sound while you move your arm like an elephant's trunk: /e/ /e/ elephant.*

Repeat after me: /e/ /e/ engine, /e/ /e/ envelope, /e/ /e/ elbow.

> Make sure that you are pronouncing the short E, as in *elephant*, not the long E, as in *eagle*.

5. Practice blending skills.

Say: *I'll say three sounds and I want you to put them together to make a word: /e/ /n/ /d/, /n/ /e/ /t/, /b/ /e/ /d/.*

Excellent Eggs

Color each egg with the letter E.

Find the First Sound

Circle the letter that you hear at the beginning of each picture. Some pictures start with E. Some pictures start with other letters that you know.

Letter W

1. Review.

Look back at the letter E in the previous lesson. Practice /e/ /e/ elephant while making the elephant trunk motion.

2. Share the objective.

Say: *Today we'll learn what letter W looks like and sounds like.*

3. Teach the letter shape.

Point to the letters. Say: *This is letter W. There is a big W and a little W. Can you trace the two letters with your finger?*

4. Teach the letter sound.

Say: *The letter W makes the sound /w/, like at the beginning of watch. Let's make the W sound while you tap your wrist like you're pointing to a watch: /w/ /w/ watch.*

Repeat after me: /w/ /w/ whale, /w/ /w/ window, /w/ /w/ watermelon.

5. Practice identifying beginning sounds.

I'll say three words and I want you to tell me which one doesn't start with W: win, pen, wish. Let's try again: turn, wash, week.

Watch for W

Circle each letter W.

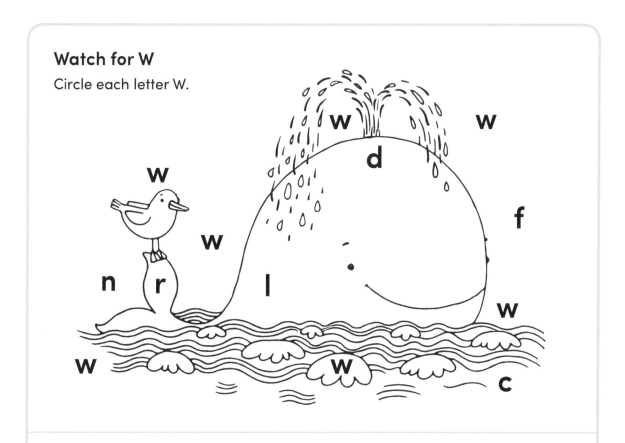

Where Are the W Words?

Draw a line from each picture that starts with W to a letter W.

W   W   W   W

Blending Known Letters

1. Review.

Say: *Can you remember the sound and shape for each of these letters?*

2. Share the objective.

Say: *Today you will learn how to blend sounds that you know to make words.*

3. Demonstrate blending sounds.

Say: *Watch how I put my finger on each dot and make the sound of the letter. Listen to how I slide through the sounds to make a word.*

Slowly run your finger across the arrow and say /wwweeeb/. Repeat this motion and sound a couple of times more quickly until you are saying the word *web* at a normal speed.

Repeat this process with the word *kit*.

4. Guide the practice.

Have the child point to each dot under the word *web* and say the individual letter sounds. Then have them move their finger across the arrow, sliding through all the sounds to make a word. Repeat with the word *kit*.

Silly Spellings

Blend the letters together to read the words. Circle the word that correctly labels the picture.

w i n   w i g   l i d   k i d

v e t   w e t   b a g   b e g

The -et Word Family

1. Review.

Say: *Can you remember the sounds for the letters E and T? Can you slide your finger across the arrow and blend the sounds together?*

2. Share the objective.

Say: *Today you will learn how to read words that end with /et/.*

3. Demonstrate reading new words with -et.

Say: *Watch how I can read more words by putting different sounds in front of /et/.*

Touch the dot under the B in *bet* and say /b/, then slide your finger across the short arrow and say /et/. Slide your finger across the long arrow and say "bet."

Have the child try blending *bet*. Repeat this process with *let*.

4. Practice rhyming skills.

Say: *I will say two words and I want you to tell me if they rhyme: yet, jet. How about get and man? How about met and pig?*

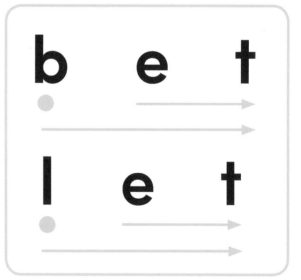

Let's Race!

Read each word around the racetrack. Can you do it again, faster? Color a star for each time you read all the way around the track.

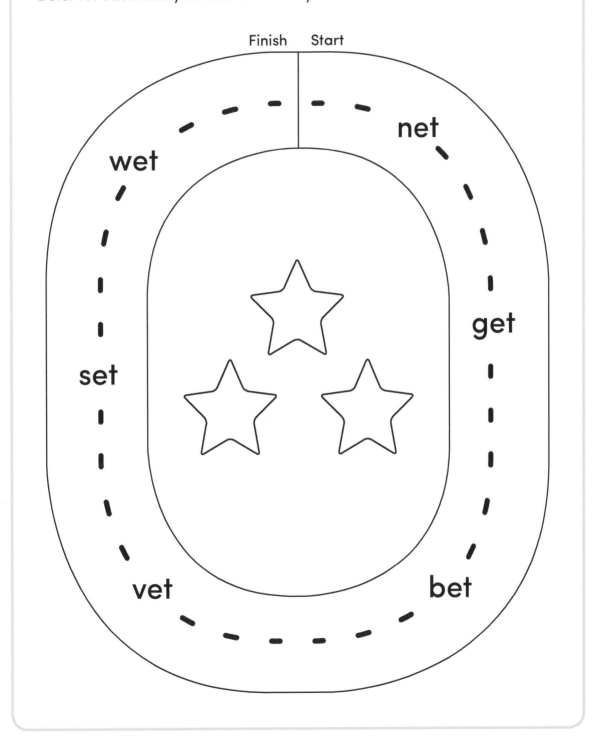

Finish   Start

net

wet

get

set

vet   bet

Letter J

1. Review.

Practice reading the -et family words in the previous lesson.

2. Share the objective.

Say: *Today we'll learn what letter J looks like and sounds like.*

3. Teach the letter shape.

Point to the letters. Say: *This is letter J. There is a big J and a little J. Can you draw the letters on the floor with your foot?*

4. Teach the letter sound.

Say: *The letter J makes the sound /j/, like at the beginning of jump rope. Let's make the J sound while you pretend you're swinging a jump rope: /j/ /j/ jump rope.*

Repeat after me: /j/ /j/ jet, /j/ /j/ jar, /j/ /j/ jacket.

5. Practice identifying beginning sounds.

Say: *I'll say a word and I want you to tell me the beginning sound: jam. How about mix? How about jump?*

Connect the Js

Connect the letter Js to get through the maze.

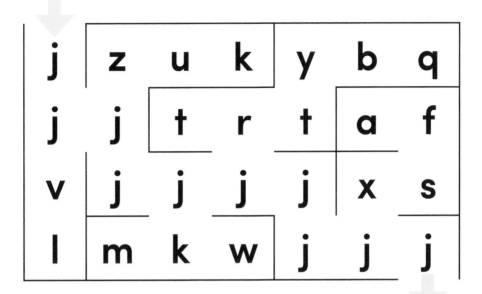

Find the First Sound

Circle the letter that you hear at the beginning of each picture. Some pictures start with J. Some pictures start with other letters that you know.

Letter P

1. Review.

Look back at the letter J in the previous lesson. Practice /j/ /j/ jump rope while pretending to swing a jump rope.

2. Share the objective.

Say: *Today we'll learn what letter P looks like and sounds like.*

3. Teach the letter shape.

Point to the letters. Say: *This is letter P. There is a big P and a little P. Can you trace the two letters with your finger?*

4. Teach the letter sound.

Say: *The letter P makes the sound /p/, like at the beginning of plane. Let's make the P sound while you put your arms out like airplane wings: /p/ /p/ plane.*

Repeat after me: /p/ /p/ penguin, /p/ /p/ popcorn, /p/ /p/ pencil.

> Pronounce the P sound as a short puff of air. Avoid adding a vowel sound at the end ("puh").

5. Practice blending skills.

Say: *I'll say three sounds and I want you to put them together to make a word: /p/ /i/ /g/, /p/ /e/ /n/, /p/ /e/ /t/.*

Three in a Row

Draw lines to connect three letter Ps in a row. The lines can be vertical, horizontal, or diagonal.

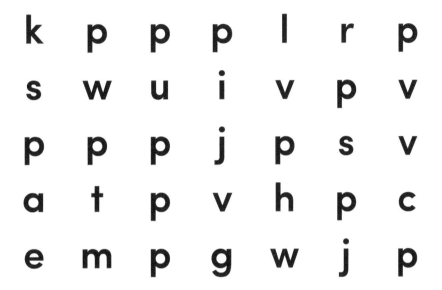

k p p p l r p

s w u i v p v

p p p j p s v

a t p v h p c

e m p g w j p

Circle the Picture

Circle the pictures that begin with P.

Letter Y

1. Review.

Look back at the letter P in the previous lesson. Practice /p/ /p/ plane with outstretched arms like airplane wings.

2. Share the objective.

Say: *Today we'll learn what letter Y looks like and sounds like.*

3. Teach the letter shape.

Point to the letters. Say: *This is letter Y. There is a big Y and a little Y. Can you write the letters in the air with a pretend magic wand?*

4. Teach the letter sound.

Say: *The letter Y makes the sound /y/, like at the beginning of yo-yo. Let's make the Y sound while you pretend to use a yo-yo: /y/ /y/ yo-yo.*

Repeat after me: /y/ /y/ yarn, /y/ /y/ yawn, /y/ /y/ yak.

5. Practice identifying beginning sounds.

Say: *I'll say three words and I want you to tell me which one doesn't start with Y: red, you, yell. Let's try again: yes, yet, like.*

Where Is Y?

Color the boxes with the letter Y to make a path for the cat to get to the yarn.

	y	y	k	a	l
d	m	y	f	s	h
e	g	y	y	y	

Connect to the Center

Draw a line from each item that starts with Y to the letters in the center.

Yy

Letter X

1. Review.

Look back at the letter Y in the previous lesson. Practice /y/ /y/ yo-yo while pretending to use a yo-yo.

2. Share the objective.

Say: *Today we'll learn what letter X looks like and sounds like.*

3. Teach the letter shape.

Point to the letters. Say: *This is letter X. There is a big X and a little X. Can you make the X shape with your hands?*

4. Teach the letter sound.

Say: *The letter X makes the sound /x/, like at the end of ax. Let's make the X sound while you pretend to chop a tree with an ax: /x/ /x/ ax.*

Listen for the X sound at the end of each word. Repeat after me: fox, box, mix.

Pronounce the X as a blend of the K and S sounds ("ksss").

5. Practice blending skills.

Say: *I'll say three sounds and I want you to put them together to make a word: /s/ /i/ /x/, /t/ /u/ /x/, /w/ /a/ /x/.*

Find Letter X

Circle each letter X.

Where Are the X Words?

Draw a line from each picture to the matching word.

f i x

b o x

w a x

o x

Blending Known Letters

1. Review.

Say: *Can you remember the sound and shape for each of these letters?*

2. Share the objective.

Say: *Today you will learn how to blend sounds that you know to make words.*

3. Demonstrate blending sounds.

Say: *Watch how I put my finger on each dot and make the sound of the letter. Listen to how I slide through the sounds to make a word.*

Slowly run your finger across the arrow and say /paaannn/. Repeat this motion and sound a couple of times more quickly until you are saying the word *pan* at a normal speed.

Repeat this process with the word *yet.*

4. Guide the practice.

Have the child point to each dot under the word *pan* and say the individual letter sounds. Then have them move their finger across the arrow, sliding through all the sounds to make a word. Repeat with the word *yet.*

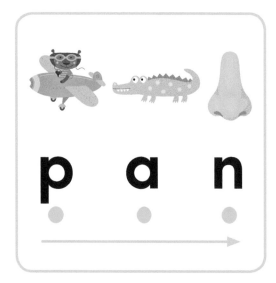

Blend and Match

Touch the dots and say each sound in the first word. Then slide through the sounds to blend them into a word. Draw a line to connect each word to the matching picture.

p o t

j o g

y u m

j a m

b o x

The -it Word Family

1. Review.

Say: *Can you remember the sounds for the letters I and T? Can you slide your finger across the arrow and blend the sounds together?*

2. Share the objective.

Say: *Today you will learn how to read words that end with /it/.*

3. Demonstrate reading new words with -it.

Say: *Watch how I can read more words by putting different sounds in front of /it/.*

Touch the dot under the B in *bit* and say /b/, then slide your finger across the short arrow and say /it/. Slide your finger across the long arrow and say "bit."

Have the child try blending *bit*. Repeat this process with *fit*.

4. Practice rhyming skills.

Say: *I will say two words and I want you to tell me if they rhyme: quit, ten. How about sit and fit? How about hit and split?*

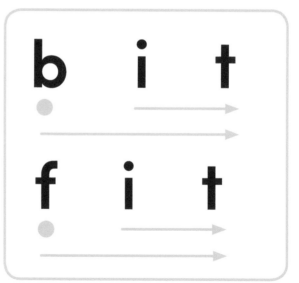

Word Family Fun

Color each circle that has a word or a picture from the -it family.

Letter Q

1. Review.

Practice reading the -it family words in the previous lesson.

2. Share the objective.

Say: *Today we'll learn what letter Q looks like and sounds like.*

3. Teach the letter shape.

Point to the letters. Say: *This is letter Q. There is a big Q and a little Q. Can you trace the two letters with your finger?*

4. Teach the letter sound.

Say: *The letter Q makes the sound /qu/, like at the beginning of queen. Let's make the Q sound while you pretend to put a crown on your head: /qu/ /qu/ queen.*

Repeat after me: /qu/ /qu/ quilt, /qu /qu/ quiet, /qu/ /qu/ quack.

5. Practice blending skills.

Say: *I'll say three sounds and I want you to put them together to make a word: /qu/ /i/ /t/, /qu/ /i/ /ck/.*

The Queen of Hearts

Color each heart with the letter Q.

Circle the Picture

Say the name of each picture. Circle the pictures that begin with Q.

Letter Z

1. Review.

Look back at the letter Q in the previous lesson. Practice /qu/ /qu/ queen while pretending to put on a crown.

2. Share the objective.

Say: *Today we'll learn what letter Z looks like and sounds like.*

3. Teach the letter shape.

Point to the letters. Say: *This is letter Z. There is a big Z and a little Z. Can you draw Z in the air with your elbow?*

4. Teach the letter sound.

Say: *The letter Z makes the sound /z/, like at the beginning of zipper. Let's make the Z sound while you pretend to zip a jacket: /z/ /z/ zipper.*

Repeat after me: /z/ /z/ zebra, /z/ /z/ zero, /z/ /z/ zigzag.

Pronounce the Z as a continuous "zzz." Avoid adding a vowel sound at the end ("zuh").

5. Practice blending skills.

Say: *I'll say three sounds and I want you to put them together to make a word: /qu/ /i/ /z/, /b/ /u/ /zz/, /f/ /u/ /zz/.*

Connect the Zs

Connect the letter Zs to get through the maze.

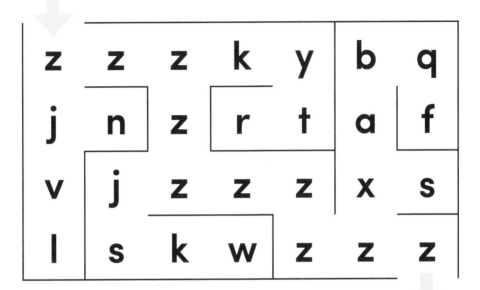

Where Are the Z Words?

Draw a line from each picture that starts with Z to a letter Z.

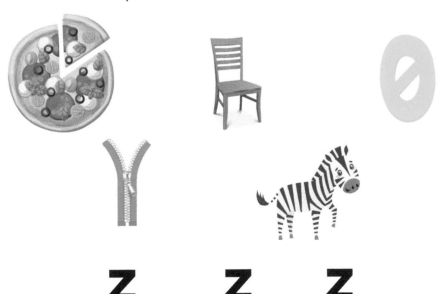

The -an Word Family

1. Review.

Say: *Can you remember the sounds for the letters A and N? Can you slide your finger across the arrow and blend the sounds together?*

2. Share the objective.

Say: *Today you will learn how to read words that end with /an/.*

3. Demonstrate reading new words with -an.

Say: *Watch how I can read more words by putting different sounds in front of /an/.*

Touch the dot under the M in *man* and say /m/, then slide your finger across the short arrow and say /an/. Slide your finger across the long arrow and say "man."

Have the child try blending *man*. Repeat this process with *fan*.

4. Practice rhyming skills.

Say: *I'll say three words and I want you to tell me which one doesn't rhyme: plan, met, tan. Let's try again: leg, pan, van.*

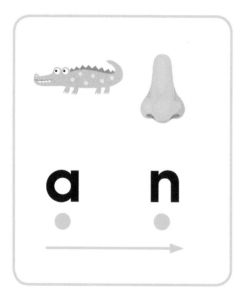

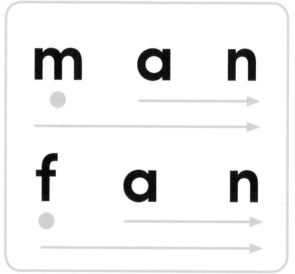

Slide Through and Circle

Say each letter sound. Blend the sounds together to make a word. Circle the picture that matches the word.

r a n

p a n

v a n

m a n

c a n

The -en Word Family

1. Review.

Say: *Can you remember the sounds for the letters E and N? Can you slide your finger across the arrow and blend the sounds together?*

2. Share the objective.

Say: *Today you will learn how to read words that end with /en/.*

3. Demonstrate reading new words with -en.

Say: *Watch how I can read more words by putting different sounds in front of /en/.*

Touch the dot under the T in *ten* and say /t/, then slide your finger across the short arrow and say /en/. Slide your finger across the long arrow and say "ten."

Have the child try blending *ten*. Repeat this process with *hen*.

4. Practice rhyming skills.

Say: *I'll say three words and I want you to tell me which one doesn't rhyme: when, then, hit. Let's try again: bad, den, pen.*

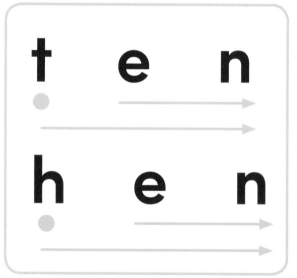

Let's Race!

Read each word around the racetrack. Can you do it again, faster? Color a star for each time you read all the way around the track.

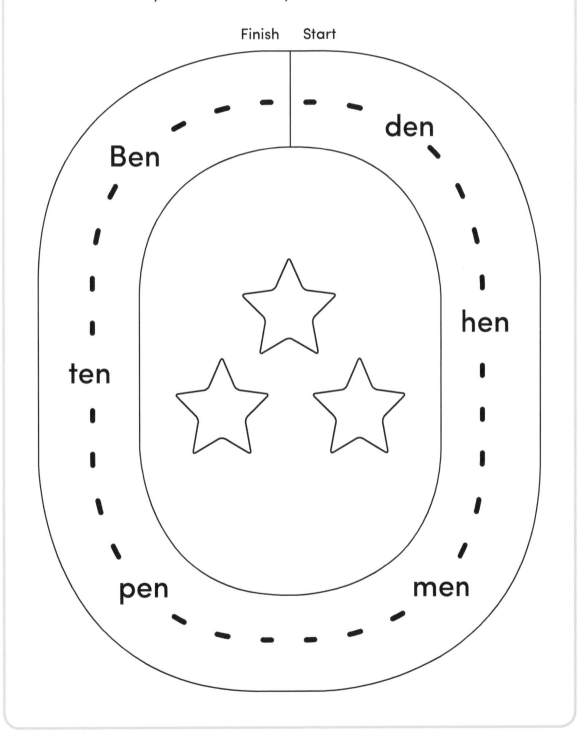

Finish   Start

den

Ben

hen

ten

pen   men

The -in Word Family

1. Review.

Say: *Can you remember the sounds for the letters I and N? Can you slide your finger across the arrow and blend the sounds together?*

2. Share the objective.

Say: *Today you will learn how to read words that end with /in/.*

3. Demonstrate reading new words with -in.

Say: *Watch how I can read more words by putting different sounds in front of /in/.*

Touch the dot under the B in *bin* and say /b/, then slide your finger across the short arrow and say /in/. Slide your finger across the long arrow and say "bin."

Have the child try blending *bin*. Repeat this process with *fin*.

4. Practice rhyming skills.

Say: *I'll say three words and I want you to tell me which one doesn't rhyme: spin, hat, thin. Let's try again: pin, tin, web.*

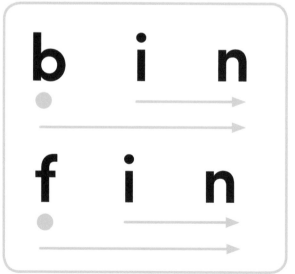

Take the Twins to the Bin

Color the boxes with words from the -in family to make a path for the twins to get to the recycling bin.

	ran	net	an
bin	it		not
tin	win	I	hen
	sin	fin	pin
bed	am	an	

Review the Word Families -an, -en, and -in

1. Share the objective.

Say: *Word families help you read a lot of words. Today we'll practice the -an, -en, and -in word families.*

2. Demonstrate reading word families.

Point to the column of -an words. Say: *Each of these words ends with /an/. Listen while I read them.*

Point to and read each word in the -an column.

3. Guide the practice.

Say: *Now you try. Point to each word as you read it.*

Repeat this process with the other two columns.

-an	-en	-in
can	men	fin
pan	den	pin
fan	pen	win

Spin and Read

Use the tip of a pencil to hold a paper clip loop to the center of the spinner. Flick the paper clip. Read the word list that the paper clip lands on. Color a star for each list that you read.

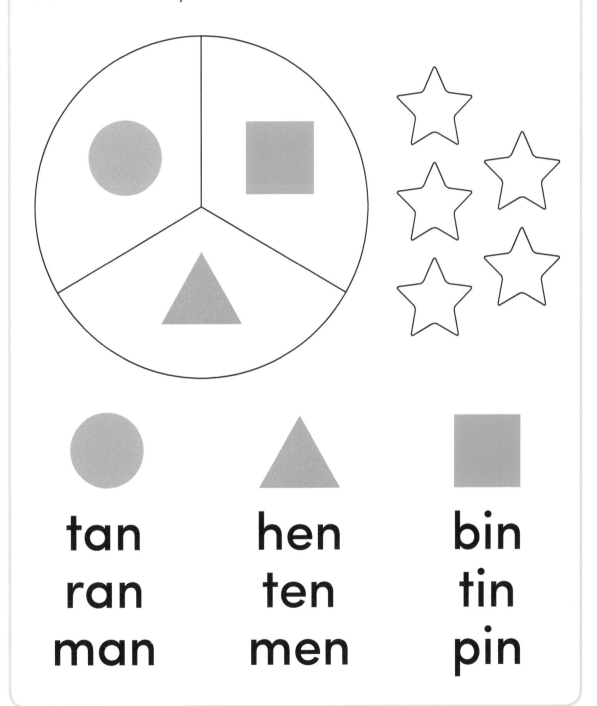

tan
ran
man

hen
ten
men

bin
tin
pin

Sight Words *I* and *a*

1. Share the objective.

Say: *Today you will learn two new words:* I and a.

2. Demonstrate reading the new words.

Say: *These two words are easy because they're each only one letter long.*

Point to each word and say: *This is the word* I *and this is the word* a. *Watch how I read them in a sentence.*

Touch the dot under each word as you read the first sentence.

> Touching the dots under the words reinforces the concept of tracking print from left to right and also one-to-one correspondence between printed and spoken words.

3. Guide the practice.

Say: *Now you try touching the dots and reading each sentence.*

> If the child needs more support, have them touch the dots while you read the sentence together a few times.

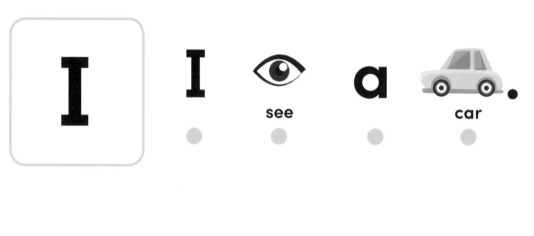

 see

 nest

Picture Reading

Touch the dot under each word while you read the sentences. Color in the star when you finish each one.

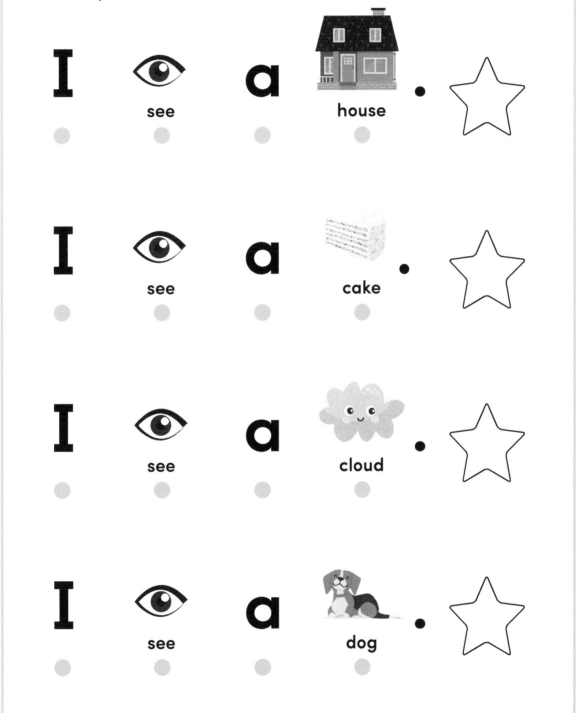

I ● see ● a ● house ●

I ● see ● a ● cake ●

I ● see ● a ● cloud ●

I ● see ● a ● dog ●

Sight Word *am*

1. Review.

Practice reading the words *I* and *a* from the previous lesson.

2. Share the objective.

Say: *Today you will learn the word* am.

3. Demonstrate reading the new word.

Say: *This is the word* am. *Watch how I read it in a sentence.*

Touch the dot under each word as you read the first sentence.

4. Guide the practice.

Say: *Now you try touching the dots and reading each sentence.*

Am is a word that can be sounded out, but it is used so frequently that it is better for children to memorize it as a whole word by sight.

I   am      .

happy

I   am      .

tired

Fish Frenzy

Color each fish with the word *am*.

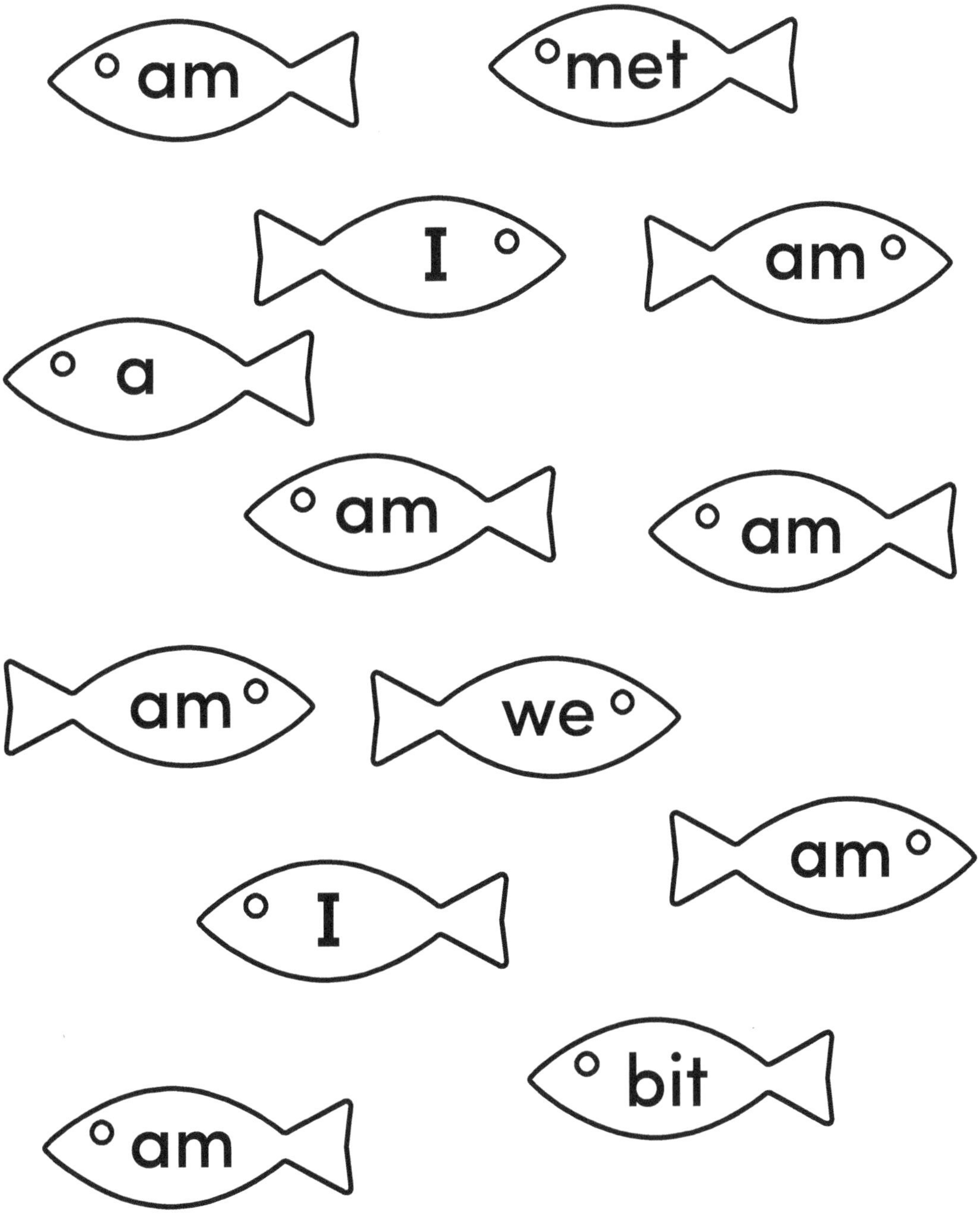

am

°met

I

am°

a

am

am

am°

we°

I

am°

bit

°am

The -ip Word Family

1. Review.

Say: *Can you remember the sounds for the letters I and P? Can you slide your finger across the arrow and blend the sounds together?*

2. Share the objective.

Say: *Today you will learn how to read words that end with /ip/.*

3. Demonstrate reading new words with -ip.

Say: *Watch how I can read more words by putting different sounds in front of /ip/.*

Touch the dot under the H in *hip* and say /h/, then slide your finger across the short arrow and say /ip/. Slide your finger across the long arrow and say "hip."

Have the child try blending *hip*. Repeat this process with *sip*.

4. Practice rhyming skills.

Say: *I'll say three words and I want you to tell me which one doesn't rhyme: ship, slip, get. Let's try again: name, flip, clip.*

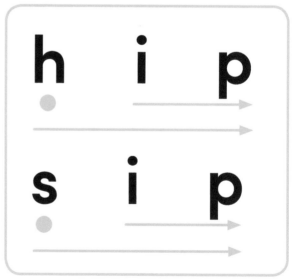

Silly Spellings

Blend the letters together to read the words. Circle the word that correctly labels the picture.

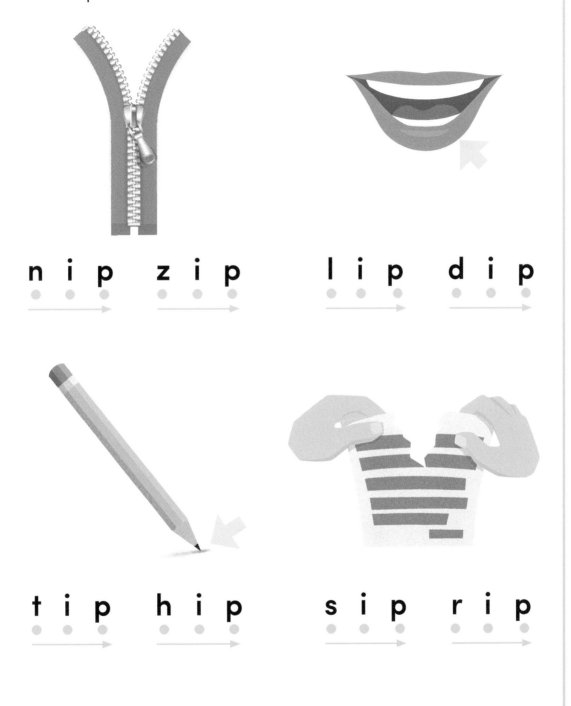

n i p   z i p

l i p   d i p

t i p   h i p

s i p   r i p

The -ug Word Family

1. Review.

Say: *Can you remember the sounds for the letters U and G? Can you slide your finger across the arrow and blend the sounds together?*

2. Share the objective.

Say: *Today you will learn how to read words that end with /ug/.*

3. Demonstrate reading new words with -ug.

Say: *Watch how I can read more words by putting different sounds in front of /ug/.*

Touch the dot under the D in *dug* and say /d/, then slide your finger across the short arrow and say /ug/. Slide your finger across the long arrow and say "dug."

Have the child try blending *dug*. Repeat this process with *lug*.

4. Practice rhyming skills.

Say: *Can you think of more words that rhyme with dug and lug?*

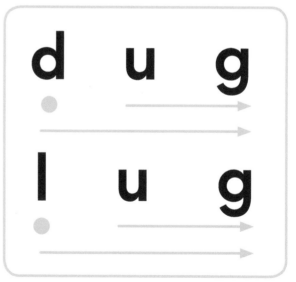

Blend and Match

Blend the sounds together to read each word. Draw lines to connect each word to the correct picture.

b u g

r u g

m u g

j u g

h u g

The -ap Word Family

1. Review.

Say: *Can you remember the sounds for the letters A and P? Can you slide your finger across the arrow and blend the sounds together?*

2. Share the objective.

Say: *Today you will learn how to read words that end with /ap/.*

3. Demonstrate reading new words with -ap.

Say: *Watch how I can read more words by putting different sounds in front of /ap/.*

Touch the dot under the G in *gap* and say /g/, then slide your finger across the short arrow and say /ap/. Slide your finger across the long arrow and say "gap."

Have the child try blending *gap*. Repeat this process with *lap*.

4. Practice rhyming skills.

Say: *Can you think of more words that rhyme with gap and lap?*

Find the Cap

Color the boxes with words from the -ap family to help the boy get to his cap. Read the -ap words.

	tap	net	I
a	zap	map	dot
an		nap	hit
can	jam	sap	
	gap	rap	man

Review the Word Families -ip, -ug, and -ap

1. Share the objective.

Say: *Today we'll practice the -ip, -ug, and -ap word families.*

2. Demonstrate reading word families.

Point to the column of -ip words. Say: *Each of these words ends with /ip/. Listen while I read them.*

3. Guide the practice.

Say: *Now you try. Point to each word as you read it.*

Repeat this process with the other two columns.

-ip	-ug	-ap
dip	bug	nap
hip	hug	lap
lip	mug	map

Blast Off with Word Families

Use the code to color the picture. Choose any color for areas that do not have a word.

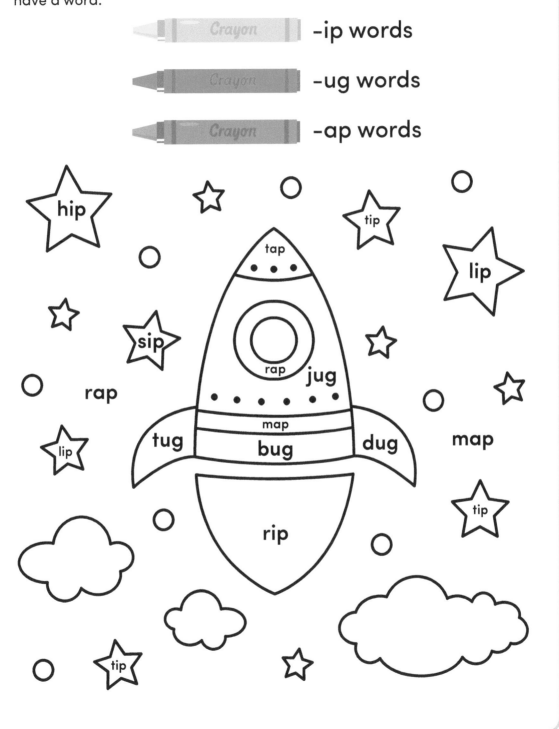

☐ Crayon — -ip words

☐ Crayon — -ug words

☐ Crayon — -ap words

hip
tip
lip
tap
sip
rap
jug
rap
tug
map
bug
dug
map
lip
rip
tip
tip

Sight Word *have*

1. Share the objective.

Say: *Today you will learn the word* have.

2. Demonstrate reading the new word.

Point to the word and say: *This is the word* have. *The letters don't make their normal sounds, so we just have to memorize what the word looks like. Watch how I read it in a sentence.*

Touch the dot under each word as you read the first sentence.

3. Guide the practice.

Say: *Now you try touching the dots and reading each sentence.*

have

I have  . 
candy

●　　　●　　　●

I have 👓 .
glasses

●　　　●　　　●

Camping Picture Reading

Touch the dot under each word while you read the sentences. Color in the star when you finish each one.

I have a 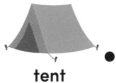 .

tent

I have a  .

flashlight

I have a  .

jacket

I have a  .

chair

Sight Word *we*

1. Review.

Look back at the previous lesson and practice reading the word *have*.

2. Share the objective.

Say: *Today you will learn the word* we.

3. Demonstrate reading the new word.

Point to the word and say: *This is the word* we. *Watch how I read it in a sentence.*

Touch the dot under each word as you read the first sentence.

You may want to point out that the upper-case W is used in the examples because it's the very first letter in the sentence.

4. Guide the practice.

Say: *Now you try touching the dots and reading each sentence.*

we

We have .

pizza

We have .

presents

Wheel of Words

Use the tip of a pencil to hold a paper clip loop to the center of the spinner. Flick the paper clip. Read the word that the paper clip lands on. Cover a matching word on the grid with some kind of marker (cereal piece, coin, scrap of paper, etc.). See how quickly you can cover them all.

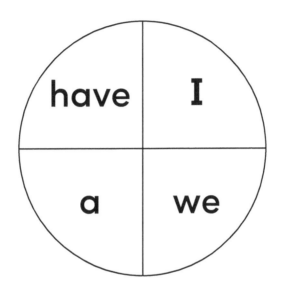

we	I	have	a
a	have	we	a
I	we	a	have
have	a	I	we

The bl Blend

1. Review.

Look back at the previous lesson and practice reading the word *we*.

2. Share the objective.

Say: *Today you will learn how to read words that start with the sound /bl/.*

3. Demonstrate reading the blend.

Say: *There are many words that start with the letters B and L next to each other. We could say the sound of each letter by itself like this, /b/ /l/, but it's faster to blend the two letters together and always remember that B and L say /bl/.*

Listen for the /bl/ sound at the beginning of these words.

Point to each picture and read the words.

4. Guide the practice.

Say: *Can you circle the B-L at the beginning of each of these words?*

> Consonant blends are similar to word family patterns in that they are chunks that children learn to recognize in words.

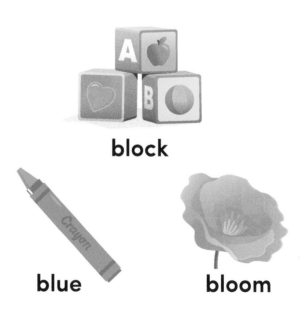

block

blue

bloom

Blend Blackout

Color each circle that has a word or picture that starts with the /bl/ sound. Practice reading the /bl/ words.

The cl Blend

1. Review.

Look back at the previous lesson and practice naming the pictures that start with the bl blend.

2. Share the objective.

Say: *Today you will learn how to read words that start with the sound /cl/.*

3. Demonstrate reading the blend.

Say: *There are many words that start with the letters C and L next to each other. We could say the sound of each letter by itself like this, /c/ /l/, but it's faster to blend the two letters together and always remember that C and L say /cl/.*

Listen for the /cl/ sound at the beginning of these words.

Point to each picture and read the words.

4. Guide the practice.

Say: *Can you circle the C-L at the beginning of each of these words?*

clock

clown

cloud

Silly Spellings

Blend the letters together to read the words. Circle the word that correctly labels the picture.

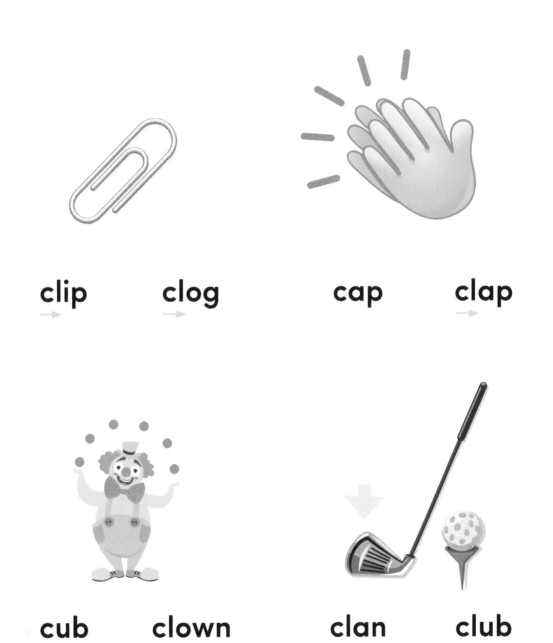

clip   clog   cap   clap

cub   clown   clan   club

The fl Blend

1. Review.

Look back at the previous lesson and practice naming the pictures that start with the cl blend.

2. Share the objective.

Say: *Today you will learn how to read words that start with the sound /fl/.*

3. Demonstrate reading the blend.

Say: *The letters F and L together sound like /fl/. We could say the sound of each letter by itself like this, /f/ /l/, but it's faster to blend the two letters together and always remember that F and L say /fl/.*

Listen for the /fl/ sound at the beginning of these words.

Point to each picture and read the words.

4. Guide the practice.

Say: *Can you circle the F-L at the beginning of each of these words?*

flamingo

flower

flame

Blend and Match

Slide through the sounds to blend them into a word. Draw a line to connect each word to the matching picture

flap

flag

flex

flat

flip

Review the Blends
bl, cl, and fl

1. Share the objective.

Say: *Today we'll practice the B-L, C-L, and F-L blends.*

2. Demonstrate the sound of each blend.

Point to the picture of blocks.

Say: *The letters B and L together sound like /bl/, as in blocks.*

3. Guide the practice.

Say: *What other words can you think of that start with the /bl/ sound?*

Repeat steps 2 and 3 with the picture of clapping hands and the picture of a flower.

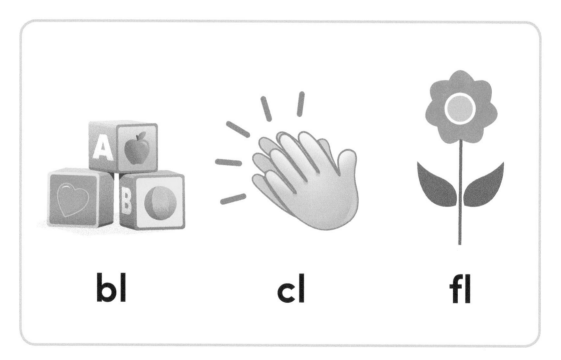

bl   **cl**   **fl**

Spin and Go

Choose something to mark your place, like a coin or a piece of cereal, and put it on the start arrow. Use the tip of a pencil to hold a paper clip loop to the center of the spinner. Flick the paper clip. Move forward to the next picture that matches the blend on the spinner. How fast can you get to the end of the path?

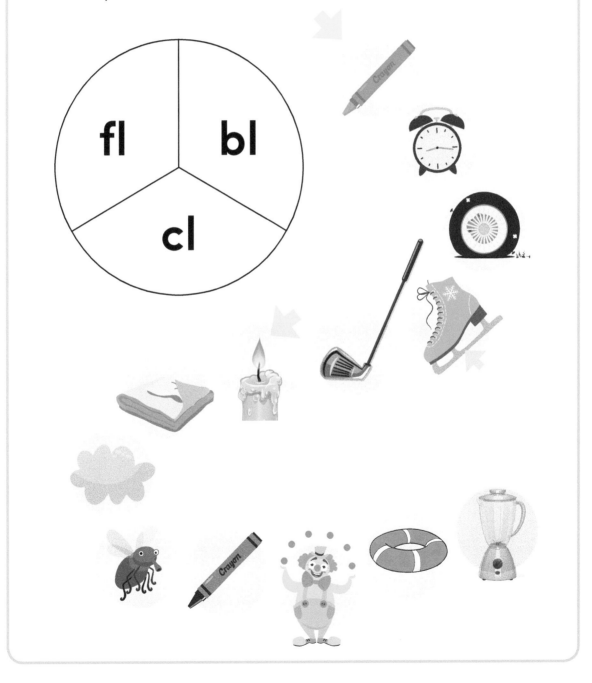

Sight Word *the*

1. Share the objective.

Say: *Today you will learn the word* the.

2. Demonstrate reading the new word.

Point to the word and say: *This is the word* the. *The letters don't make their normal sounds, so we just have to memorize what the word looks like. Watch how I read it in a sentence.*

Touch the dot under each word as you read the first sentence.

3. Guide the practice.

Say: *Now you try touching the dots and reading each sentence.*

I am the  .

duck

•   •   •   •

I am the  .

lion

•   •   •   •

Search the Park

Circle the word *the* every time you see it.

Sight Word *is*

1. Review.

Look back at the previous lesson and practice reading the word *the*.

2. Share the objective.

Say: *Today you will learn the word* is.

3. Demonstrate reading the new word.

Point to the word and say: *This is the word* is. *Watch how I read it in a sentence.*

Touch the dot under each word as you read the first sentence.

4. Guide the practice.

Say: *Now you try touching the dots and reading each sentence.*

is

He   is   swinging .

She   is   running .

Celebrate Word Families

Use the code to color the picture. Choose any color for areas that do not have a word.

is   we

the   have

The gl Blend

1. Review.

Look back at the previous lesson and practice reading the word *is*.

2. Share the objective.

Say: *Today you will learn how to read words that start with the sound /gl/.*

3. Demonstrate reading the blend.

Say: *The letters G and L together sound like /gl/. Listen for the /gl/ sound at the beginning of these words.*

Point to each picture and read the words.

4. Guide the practice.

Say: *Can you circle the G-L at the beginning of each of these words?*

5. Practice blending skills.

Say: *I'll say two or three sounds and I want you to put them together to make a word: /gl/ /o/ /p/, /gl/ /ow/, /gl/ /a/ /d/.*

glove

glass

glue

Connect to the Center

Draw a line from each item that starts with /gl/ to the letters in the center.

The pl Blend

1. Review.

Look back at the previous lesson and practice naming the pictures that start with the gl blend.

2. Share the objective.

Say: *Today you will learn how to read words that start with the sound /pl/.*

3. Demonstrate reading the blend.

Say: *The letters P and L together sound like /pl/. Listen for the /pl/ sound at the beginning of these words.*

Point to each picture and read the words.

4. Guide the practice.

Say: *Can you circle the P-L at the beginning of each of these words?*

5. Practice blending skills.

Say: *I'll say two or three sounds and I want you to put them together to make a word: /pl/ /ay/, /pl/ /u/ /g/, /pl/ /a/ /n/.*

plant

planet

plate

Color the Blend

Color each item that starts with /pl/.

The sl Blend

1. Review.

Look back at the previous lesson and practice naming the pictures that start with the pl blend.

2. Share the objective.

Say: *Today you will learn how to read words that start with the sound /sl/.*

3. Demonstrate reading the blend.

Say: *The letters S and L together sound like /sl/. Listen for the /sl/ sound at the beginning of these words.*

Point to each picture and read the words.

4. Guide the practice.

Say: *Can you circle the S-L at the beginning of each of these words?*

5. Practice identifying beginning sounds.

Say: *I'll say a word and I want you to tell me if it starts with /sl/: slop. How about sling? How about gray?*

sleep

slide

slippers

Blend and Match

Slide through the sounds to blend them into a word. Draw a line to connect each word to the matching picture.

slip →

slam →

slug →

sled →

slap →

Review the Blends gl, pl, and sl

1. Share the objective.

Say: *Today we'll practice the G-L, P-L, and S-L blends.*

2. Demonstrate the sound of each blend.

Point to the picture of glasses.

Say: *The letters G and L together sound like /gl/, as in glasses.*

3. Guide the practice.

Say: *What other words can you think of that start with the sound /gl/?*

Repeat steps 2 and 3 with the picture of a planet and the picture of a slide.

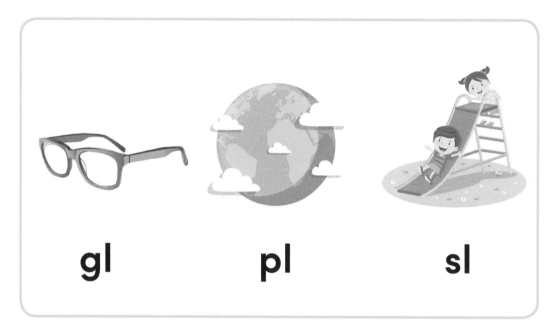

| gl | pl | sl |

Circle the Picture

Say each blend. Circle the picture(s) in the row that match the blend.

pl

gl

sl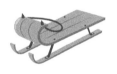

fl

cl

Sight Word *are*

1. Share the objective.

Say: *Today you will learn the word* are.

2. Demonstrate reading the new word.

Point to the two versions of the word *are* and say: *Both of these words say "are." One starts with a big A and the other starts with a small A. The letters don't make their normal sounds, so we just have to memorize what the word looks like. Watch how I read it in a sentence.*

Touch the dot under each word as you read the first sentence.

3. Guide the practice.

Say: *Now you try touching the dots and reading each sentence.*

Are   We are  .
   happy

are   We are  .
   reading

Wheel of Words

Use the tip of a pencil to hold a paper clip loop to the center of the spinner. Flick the paper clip. Read the word that the paper clip lands on. Cover a matching word on the grid with some kind of marker (cereal piece, coin, scrap of paper). See how quickly you can cover them all.

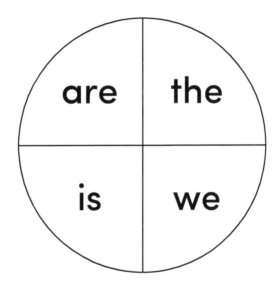

are	is	we	the
we	the	are	is
is	are	the	we
the	we	is	are

Sight Word *you*

1. Review.

Look back at the previous lesson and practice reading the word *are*.

2. Share the objective.

Say: *Today you will learn the word* you.

3. Demonstrate reading the new word.

Point to the two versions of the word *you* and say: *Both of these words say "you." One starts with a big Y and the other starts with a small Y. Watch how I read it in a sentence.*

Touch the dot under each word as you read the first sentence.

4. Guide the practice.

Say: *Now you try touching the dots and reading each sentence.*

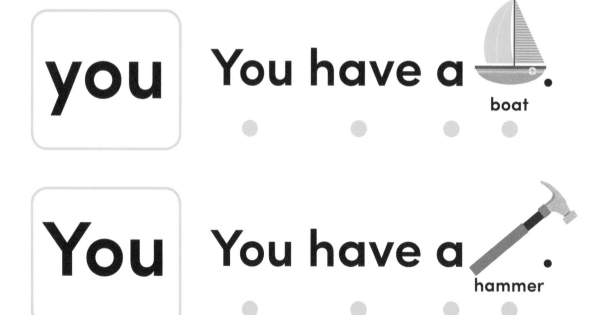

you   You have a 🚤.
                    boat

You   You have a 🔨.
                    hammer

Picture Reading

Touch the dot under each word while you read the sentences. Color in the star when you finish each one.

You are .
strong

You are . 
messy

Are you ?
scared

Are you ? 
tired

The –id Word Family

1. Review.

Say: *Can you touch each letter in this word family and tell me the sound? Can you slide your finger across the arrow and blend the sounds together?*

2. Share the objective.

Say: *Today you will learn how to read words that end with /id/.*

3. Demonstrate reading new words with -id.

Say: *Watch how I can read more words by putting different sounds in front of /id/.*

Touch the dot under the D in *did* and say /d/, then slide your finger across the short arrow and say /id/. Slide your finger across the long arrow and say "did."

Have the child try blending *did*. Repeat this process with the word *hid*.

4. Practice rhyming skills.

Say: *I'll say three words and I want you to tell me which one doesn't rhyme: kid, slid, hot. Let's try again: grid, then, rid.*

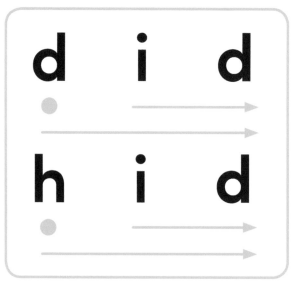

Let's Race!

Read each word around the racetrack. Can you do it again, faster? Color a star for each time you read all the way around the track.

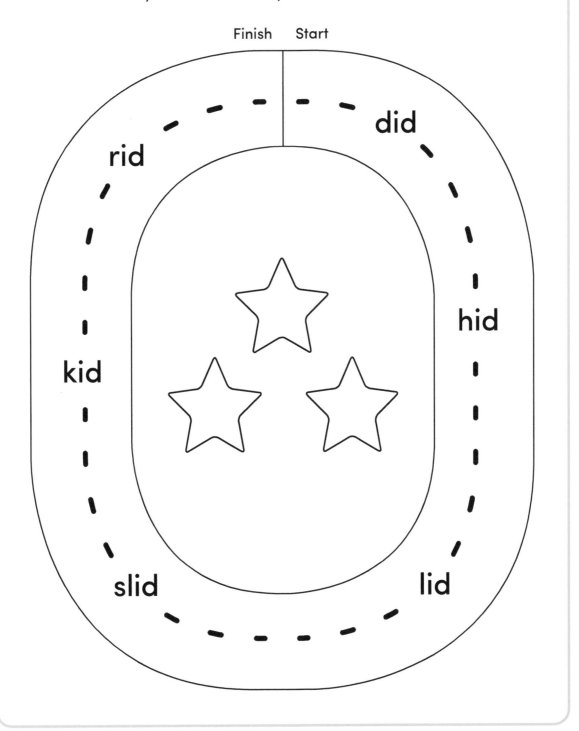

Finish Start

did

hid

rid

kid

lid

slid

The -op Word Family

1. Review.

Say: *Can you touch each letter in this word family and tell me the sound? Can you slide your finger across the arrow and blend the sounds together?*

2. Share the objective.

Say: *Today you will learn how to read words that end with /op/.*

3. Demonstrate reading new words with -op.

Say: *Watch how I can read more words by putting different sounds in front of /op/.*

Touch the dot under the H in *hop* and say /h/, then slide your finger across the short arrow and say /op/. Slide your finger across the long arrow and say "hop."

4. Guide the practice.

Say: *Now you try blending this word.*

Repeat this process with the word *pop*.

5. Practice blending skills.

Say: *I'll say three sounds and I want you to put them together to make a word: /sh/ /o/ /p/, /t/ /o/ /p/, /dr/ /o/ /p/.*

Slide Through and Circle

Blend the sounds together to make a word. Circle the picture that matches the word.

m o p

c o p

h o p

p o p

f l o p

The -ad Word Family

1. Review.

Say: *Can you touch each letter in this word family and tell me the sound? Can you slide your finger across the arrow and blend the sounds together?*

2. Share the objective.

Say: *Today you will learn how to read words that end with /ad/.*

3. Demonstrate reading new words with -ad.

Say: *Watch how I can read more words by putting different sounds in front of /ad/.*

Touch the dot under the B in *bad* and say /b/, then slide your finger across the short arrow and say /ad/. Slide your finger across the long arrow and say "bad."

4. Guide the practice.

Say: *Now you try blending this word.*

Repeat this process with the word *had*.

5. Practice rhyming skills.

Say: *Can you think of more words that rhyme with bad and had?*

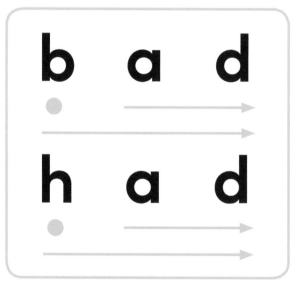

Blend and Match

Slide through the sounds to blend them into a word. Draw a line to connect each word to the matching picture.

glad

dad

sad

mad

bad

Review the Word Families -id, -op, and -ad

1. Share the objective.

Say: *Today we'll practice the -id, -op, and -ad word families.*

2. Demonstrate reading word families.

Point to the column of -id words. Say: *Each of these words ends with /id/. Listen while I read them.*

Point to and read each word in the -id column.

3. Guide the practice.

Say: *Now you try. Point to each word as you read it.*

Repeat this process with the other two columns.

4. Practice identifying ending sounds.

Say: *I'll say a word and you tell me which word family it goes with: sad, kid, shop.*

-ip	-op	-ad
kid	hop	mad
lid	mop	sad
did	pop	dad

Spin and Read

Use the tip of a pencil to hold the loop of a paper clip to the center of the spinner. Flick the paper clip. Read the word list that the paper clip lands on. Color a star for each time that you read a list.

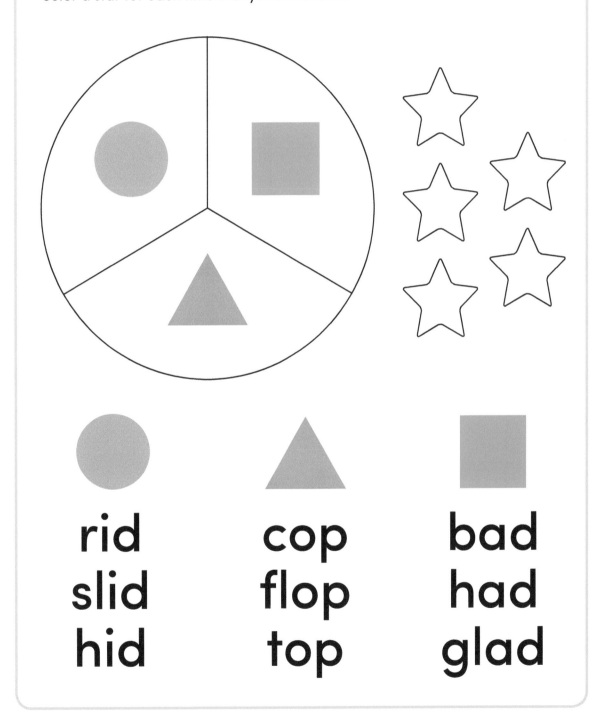

rid
slid
hid

cop
flop
top

bad
had
glad

Sight Word *and*

1. Share the objective.

Say: *Today you will learn the word* and.

2. Demonstrate reading the new word.

Say: *This is the word* and. *Watch how I use it to read about things that go together.*

Touch the dot under each word as you read the first sentence.

3. Guide the practice.

Say: *Now you try touching the dots and reading each pair.*

bacon   eggs

cookies   milk

In Search of Jelly

Color the boxes with the word *and* to get the peanut butter to the jelly.

	**and**	**net**	**am**
you	**and**	**I**	**we**
we	**and**		**a**
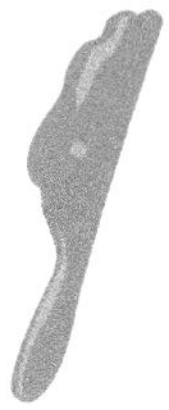	**and**	**and**	**and**
is	**I**	**you**	

Sight Word *it*

1. Review.

Look back at the previous lesson and practice reading the word *and*.

2. Share the objective.

Say: *Today you will learn the word* it.

3. Demonstrate reading the new word.

Point to the two versions of the word *it* and say: *Both of these words say "it." One starts with a big I and the other starts with a small I. Watch how I read it in a sentence.*

Touch the dot under each word as you read the first sentence.

4. Guide the practice.

Say: *Now you try touching the dots and reading each sentence.*

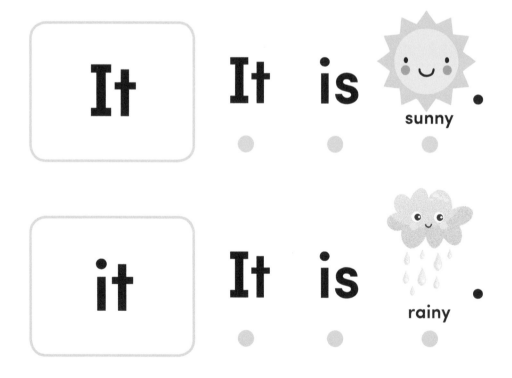

It   It is sunny.

it   It is rainy.

Search the Zoo

Circle the word *it* every time you see it.

The br Blend

1. Review.

Look back at the previous lesson and practice reading the word *it*.

2. Share the objective.

Say: *Today you will learn how to read words that start with the sound /br/.*

3. Demonstrate reading the blend.

Say: *The letters B and R together sound like /br/. Listen for the /br/ sound at the beginning of these words.*

Point to each picture and read the words.

4. Guide the practice.

Say: *Can you circle the B-R at the beginning of each of these words?*

5. Practice identifying beginning sounds.

Say: *I'll say a word and I want you to tell me if it starts with /br/: bring. How about help? How about braid?*

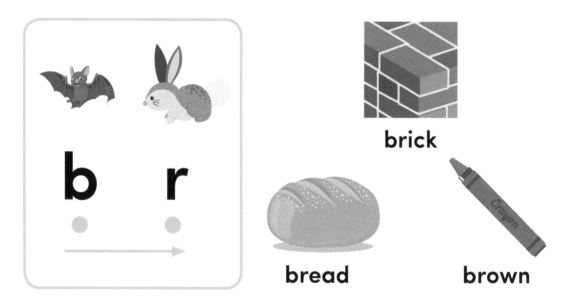

brick

bread   brown

Brighten the Bricks

Color each item that starts with /br/.

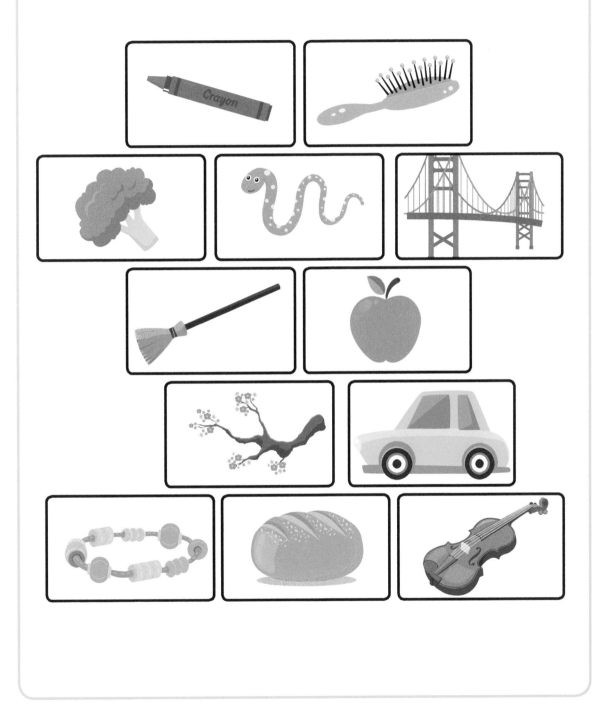

The cr Blend

1. Review.

Look back at the previous lesson and practice naming the pictures that start with the br blend.

2. Share the objective.

Say: *Today you will learn how to read words that start with the sound /cr/.*

3. Demonstrate reading the blend.

Say: *The letters C and R together sound like /cr/. Listen for the /cr/ sound at the beginning of these words.*

Point to each picture and read the words.

4. Guide the practice.

Say: *Can you circle the C-R at the beginning of each of these words?*

5. Practice identifying beginning sounds.

Say: *I'll say three words and I want you to tell me which one doesn't start with /cr/: crumb, nest, crow. Let's try again: creep, crash, boat.*

crab

cry

crown

Fill in a Face

Say the name of each picture. If it starts with /cr/, color the happy face. If it does not start with /cr/, color the sad face.

The dr Blend

1. Review.

Look back at the previous lesson and practice naming the pictures that start with the cr blend.

2. Share the objective.

Say: *Today you will learn how to read words that start with the sound /dr/.*

3. Demonstrate reading the blend.

Say: *The letters D and R together sound like /dr/. Listen for the /dr/ sound at the beginning of these words.*

Point to each picture and read the words.

4. Guide the practice.

Say: *Can you circle the D-R at the beginning of each of these words?*

5. Practice blending skills.

Say: *I'll say two or three sounds and I want you to put them together to make a word: /dr/ /u/ /m/, /dr/ /a/ /g/, /dr/ /ea/ /m/.*

d r

drill

dress

drink

Slide Through and Circle

Blend the sounds together to make a word. Circle the picture that matches the word.

drip →

drag →

drop →

drum →

Challenge Word!

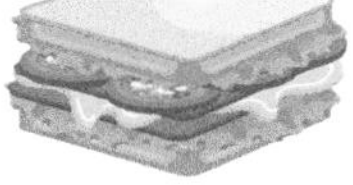

dress →

Review the Blends br, cr, and dr

1. Share the objective.

Say: *Today we'll practice the B-R, C-R, and D-R blends.*

2. Demonstrate the sound of each blend.

Point to the picture of a brick.

Say: *The letters B and R together sound like /br/, as in brick.*

3. Guide the practice.

Say: *What other words can you think of that start with the sound /br/?*

Repeat steps 2 and 3 with the picture of the crab and the picture of the drum.

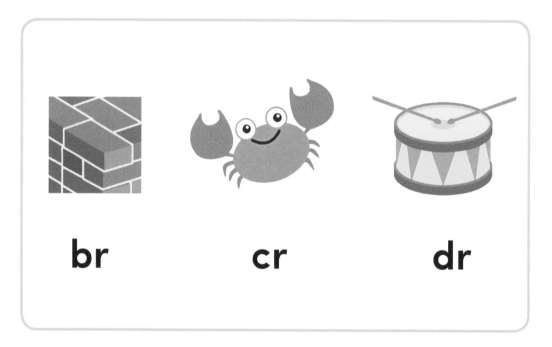

br   **cr**   **dr**

Spin and Go

Choose something to mark your place, like a coin or a piece of cereal, and put it on the start arrow. Use the tip of a pencil to hold a paper clip loop to the center of the spinner. Flick the paper clip. Move forward to the next picture that matches the blend on the spinner. How fast can you get to the end of the path?

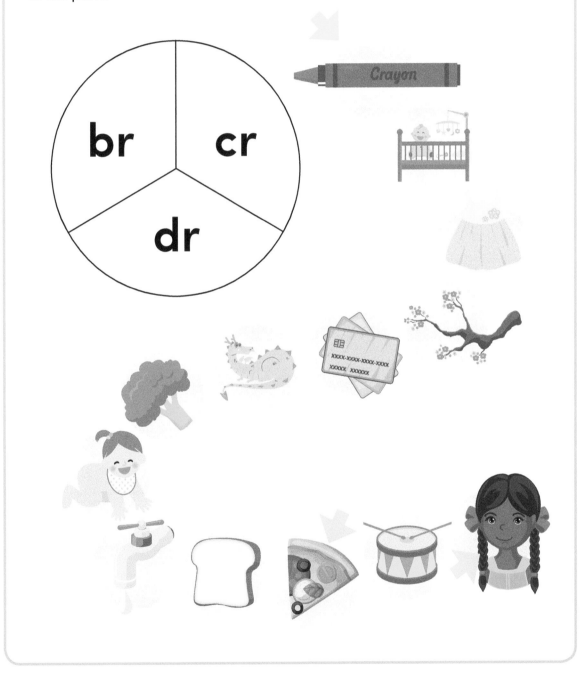

The fr Blend

1. Share the objective.

Say: *Today you will learn how to read words that start with the sound /fr/.*

2. Demonstrate reading the blend.

Say: *The letters F and R together sound like /fr/. Listen for the /fr/ sound at the beginning of these words.*

Point to each picture and read the words.

3. Guide the practice.

Say: *Can you circle the F-R at the beginning of each of these words?*

4. Practice identifying beginning sounds.

Say: *I'll say three words and I want you to tell me which one doesn't start with /fr/: free, fresh, grape. Let's try again: time, from, freckle.*

frog

fries

fruit

Connect to the Center

Draw a line from each item that starts with fr to the letters in the center.

fr

The gr Blend

1. Review.

Look back at the previous lesson and practice naming the pictures that start with the fr blend.

2. Share the objective.

Say: *Today you will learn how to read words that start with the sound /gr/.*

3. Demonstrate reading the blend.

Say: *The letters G and R together sound like /gr/. Listen for the /gr/ sound at the beginning of these words.*

Point to each picture and read the words.

4. Guide the practice.

Say: *Can you circle the G-R at the beginning of each of these words?*

5. Practice identifying beginning sounds.

Say: *I'll say a word and I want you to tell me if it starts with /gr/: water. How about grass? How about ground?*

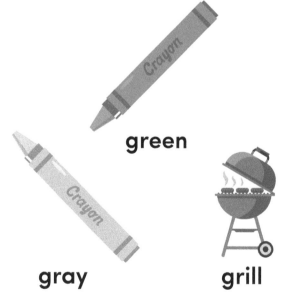

green

gray

grill

Blend Blackout

Color each circle that has a word or picture that starts with /gr/. Practice reading the /gr/ words.

The pr Blend

1. Review.

Look back at the previous lesson and practice naming the pictures that start with the gr blend.

2. Share the objective.

Say: *Today you will learn how to read words that start with the sound /pr/.*

3. Demonstrate reading the blend.

Say: *The letters P and R together sound like /pr/. Listen for the /pr/ sound at the beginning of these words.*

Point to each picture and read the words.

4. Guide the practice.

Say: *Can you circle the P-R at the beginning of each of these words?*

5. Practice blending skills.

Say: *I'll say three sounds and I want you to put them together to make a word: /pr/ /ou/ /d/, /pr/ /e/ /ss/, /pr/ /i/ /ce/.*

prince

present

printer

Fill in a Face

Say the name of each picture. If it starts with /pr/, color the happy face. If it does not start with /pr/, color the sad face.

The tr Blend

1. Review.

Look back at the previous lesson and practice naming the pictures that start with the pr blend.

2. Share the objective.

Say: *Today you will learn how to read words that start with the sound /tr/.*

3. Demonstrate reading the blend.

Say: *The letters T and R together sound like /tr/. Listen for the /tr/ sound at the beginning of these words.*

Point to each picture and read the words.

4. Guide the practice.

Say: *Can you circle the T-R at the beginning of each of these words?*

5. Practice identifying beginning sounds.

Say: *I'll say three words and I want you to tell me which one doesn't start with /tr/: train, trip, jet. Let's try again: spin, trick, trap.*

tree

t   **r**

trash

treasure

Find and Circle

Say the name of each picture. Circle the pictures that start with /tr/.

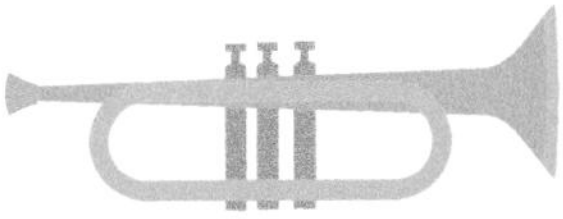

Review the Blends
fr, gr, pr, and tr

1. Share the objective.

Say: *Today we'll practice the F-R, G-R, P-R, and T-R blends.*

2. Demonstrate the sound of each blend.

Point to the picture of a frog.

Say: *The letters F and R together sound like /fr/, as in frog.*

3. Guide the practice.

Say: *What other words can you think of that start with /fr/?*

Repeat steps 2 and 3 with the pictures of the green crayon, prince, and tree.

fr

gr

pr

tr

Circle the Pictures

Say each blend. Circle the picture(s) in the row that match the blend.

fr

gr

pr

tr

br

Sight Word *in*

1. Share the objective.

Say: *Today you will learn the word* in.

2. Demonstrate reading the new word.

Point to the two versions of the word *in* and say: *Both of these words say "in." One starts with a big I and the other starts with a small I. Watch how I read it in a sentence.*

Touch the dot under each word as you read the first sentence.

3. Guide the practice.

Say: *Now you try touching the dots and reading each sentence.*

In   I am in a 🚗.
                car

in   I am in a 🏰.
                castle

Up and Away with Words!

Use the code to color the picture. Choose any color for areas that do not have a word.

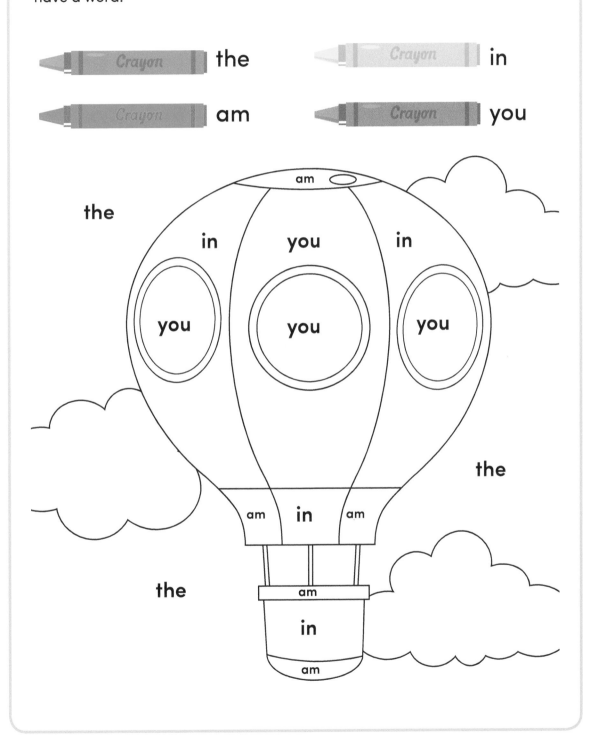

Sight Word *was*

1. Review.

Look back at the previous lesson and practice reading the word *in*.

2. Share the objective.

Say: *Today you will learn the word* was.

3. Demonstrate reading the new word.

Point to the two versions of the word *was* and say: *Both of these words say "was." One starts with a big W and the other starts with a small W. Watch how I read it in a sentence.*

Touch the dot under each word as you read the first sentence.

4. Guide the practice.

Say: *Now you try touching the dots and reading each sentence.*

Was   It was [sunny]

was   It was [rainy]

Where the Ant Went

Touch the dot under each word while you read the sentences. Color the star when you finish each one.

It was in a  .
shoe

It was in a .
flower

It was in a  .
bowl

It was in a  .
basket

The sm Blend

1. Review.

Look back at the previous lesson and practice reading the word *was*.

2. Share the objective.

Say: *Today you will learn how to read words that start with the sound /sm/.*

3. Demonstrate reading the blend.

Say: *The letters S and M together sound like /sm/. Listen for the /sm/ sound at the beginning of these words.*

Point to each picture and read the words.

4. Guide the practice.

Say: *Can you circle the S-M at the beginning of each of these words?*

5. Practice blending skills.

Say: *I'll say three sounds and I want you to put them together to make a word: /sm/ /a/ /sh/, /sm/ /a/ /ll/, /sm/ /a/ /ck/.*

s m

smile

smart

smell

Brighten the Bricks

Color each brick that has a picture that starts with sm.

The sc Blend

1. Review.

Look back at the previous lesson and practice naming the pictures that start with the sm blend.

2. Share the objective.

Say: *Today you will learn how to read words that start with the sound /sc/.*

3. Demonstrate reading the blend.

Say: *The letters S and C together sound like /sc/. Listen for the /sc/ sound at the beginning of these words.*

Point to each picture and read the words.

4. Guide the practice.

Say: *Can you circle the S-C at the beginning of each of these words?*

5. Practice identifying beginning sounds.

Say: *I'll say a word and I want you to tell me if it starts with /sc/: scoop. How about scoot? How about tree?*

scared

S   C

score

scale

Fill in a Face

Say the name of each picture. If it starts with /sc/, color the happy face. If it does not start with /sc/, color the sad face.

The st Blend

1. Review.

Look back at the previous lesson and practice naming the pictures that start with the sc blend.

2. Share the objective.

Say: *Today you will learn how to read words that start with the sound /st/.*

3. Demonstrate reading the blend.

Say: *The letters S and T together sound like /st/. Listen for the /st/ sound at the beginning of these words.*

Point to each picture and read the words.

4. Guide the practice.

Say: *Can you circle the S-T at the beginning of each of these words?*

5. Practice identifying beginning sounds.

Say: *I'll say three words and I want you to tell me which one doesn't start with /st/: stink, gap, star. Let's try again: mail, sting, step.*

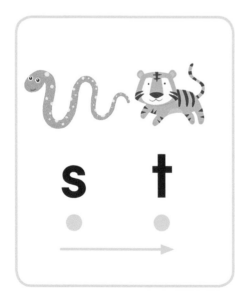

stop

stairs

storm

Connect to the Center

Draw a line from each item that starts with /st/ to the letters in the center.

st

Review the Blends sm, sc, and st

1. Share the objective.

Say: *Today we'll practice the S-M, S-C, and S-T blends.*

2. Demonstrate the sound of each blend.

Point to the picture of the smiling person.

Say: *The letters S and M together sound like /sm/, as in smile.*

3. Guide the practice.

Say: *What other words can you think of that start with the sound /sm/?*

Repeat steps 2 and 3 with the picture of the scooter and the picture of the stop sign.

4. Practice identifying beginning sounds.

Say: *I'll say a word and I want you to tell me which blend is at the beginning: small. How about stuck? How about scab?*

| sm | sc | st |

Spin and Go

Choose something to mark your place, like a coin or a piece of cereal, and put it on the start arrow. Use the tip of a pencil to hold a paper clip loop to the center of the spinner. Flick the paper clip. Move forward to the next picture that matches the blend on the spinner. How fast can you get to the end of the path?

The /ch/ Sound

1. Share the objective.

Say: *Today you will learn how to listen for words with the /ch/ sound.*

2. Demonstrate the sound of the digraph.

Say: *The letters C and H are special because they work together to make one sound. That sound is /ch/, as in cherries.*

Listen for the /ch/ sound at the beginning of these words.

Point to each picture and read the words.

> This combination is called a digraph, which means there are two letters written but only one sound. This is different from the blends, where there are two letters and both letter sounds can be heard.

3. Guide the practice.

Say: *What other words can you think of that start with /ch/?*

ch

chair

cheese

check

Help the Chick

Color the boxes with a picture that starts with /ch/ to make a path for the chick to get to the chicken coop.

Reading Words with the /ch/ Sound

1. Review.

Look back at the previous lesson and practice naming the pictures with the /ch/ sound.

2. Share the objective.

Say: *Today you will learn how to read words that start with the sound /ch/.*

3. Demonstrate reading words with /ch/.

Say: *Listen to how I say the C and H together as one sound when I read these words.*

Touch the dots while you say each sound in the word *chat*. Then slide your finger across the arrow and say the whole word. Repeat with the word *chin*.

4. Guide the practice.

Say: *Can you read the sounds and then the whole word for the last two examples?*

Let's Race!

Read each word around the racetrack. Can you do it again, faster? Color a star for each time you read all the way around the track.

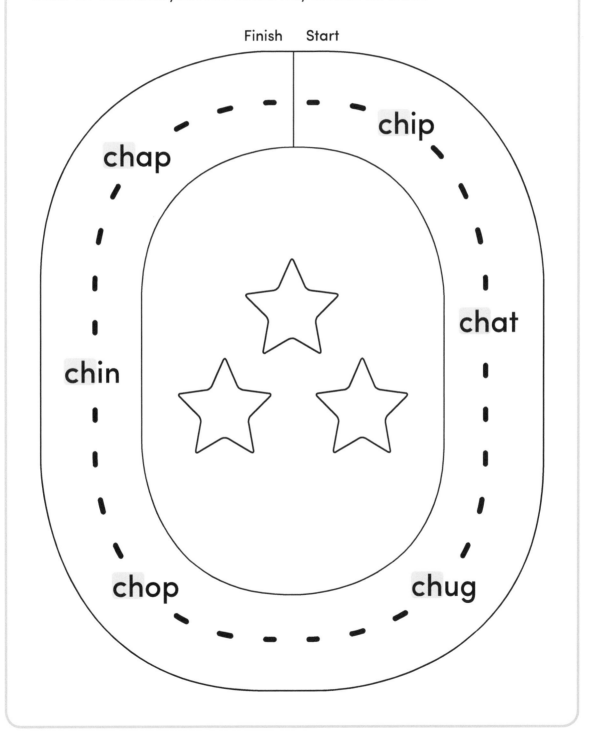

Finish   Start

chip

chap

chat

chin

chop   chug

The /th/ Sound

1. Review.

Look back at the previous lesson and practice reading some of the words with /ch/.

2. Share the objective.

Say: *Today you will learn how to listen for words with the /th/ sound.*

3. Demonstrate the sound of the digraph.

Say: *The letters T and H are special because they work together to make one sound. That sound is /th/, as in thumb.*

Listen for the /th/ in these words. Sometimes it's at the beginning of the word and other times it's at the end.

Point to each picture and read the words.

> This is only one of two sounds that the /th/ digraph makes. The other is voiced as in *them* and *this*. For simplicity, this lesson focuses on the voiceless /th/.

4. Guide the practice.

Say: *Can you circle the T-H in each of these words and then read them?*

5. Practice identifying ending sounds.

Say: *I'll say a word and you tell me if it ends with /th/: both. How about cloth? How about bend?*

th

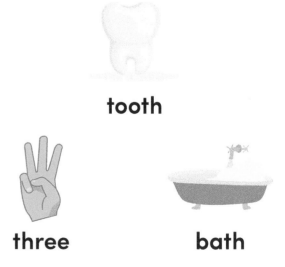

tooth

three

bath

Find and Circle

Say the name of each picture. Circle the picture(s) that have a /th/ sound at the beginning or the end.

Reading Words with the /th/ Sound

1. Review.

Look back at the previous lesson and practice naming the pictures with the /th/ sound.

2. Share the objective.

Say: *Today you will learn how to read words that have the sound /th/.*

3. Demonstrate reading words with /th/.

Say: *Listen to how I say the T and H together as one sound when I read these words.*

Touch the dots while you say each sound in the word *thin.* Then slide your finger across the arrow and say the whole word. Repeat with the word *with.*

4. Guide the practice.

Say: *Can you say the sounds and then the whole word for the last two examples?*

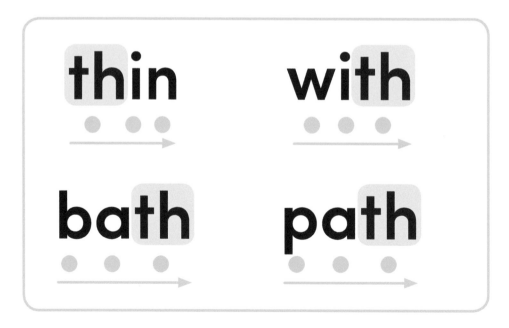

Silly Spellings

Blend the letters together to read the words. Circle the word that correctly labels the picture.

path   **thin**

math   **thud**

moth   **with**

thin   **bath**

The /sh/ Sound

1. Review.

Look back at the previous lesson and practice reading some of the words with /th/.

2. Share the objective.

Say: *Today you will learn how to listen for words with the /sh/ sound.*

3. Demonstrate the sound of the digraph.

Say: *The letters S and H are special because they work together to make one sound. That sound is /sh/, as in shark.*

Listen for the /sh/ at the beginning of these words.

Point to each picture and read the words.

4. Guide the practice.

Say: *Can you think of any other words that start with /sh/?*

5. Practice identifying ending sounds.

Say: *I'll say a word and you tell me if it ends with /sh/: wash. How about fish? How about jump?*

sh

shell

ship

shake

Fill in a Face

Say the name of each picture. If it starts with /sh/, color the happy face.
If it does not start with /sh/, color the sad face.

Reading Words with the /sh/ Sound

1. Review.

Look back at the previous lesson and practice naming the pictures with the /sh/ sound.

2. Share the objective.

Say: *Today you will learn how to read words that have the sound /sh/.*

3. Demonstrate reading words with /sh/.

Say: *Listen to how I say the S and H together as one sound when I read these words.*

Touch the dots while you say each sound in the word *shut*. Then slide your finger across the arrow and say the whole word. Repeat with the word *shop*.

4. Guide the practice.

Say: *Can you read the sounds and then the whole word for the last two examples?*

Slide Through and Circle

Blend the sounds together to make a word. Circle the picture that matches the word.

ship

shed

fish

shin

cash

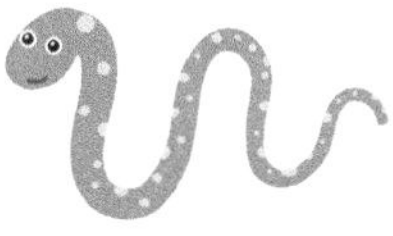

Review the Sounds /ch/, /th/, and /sh/

1. Share the objective.

Say: *Today we'll practice the /ch/, /th/, and /sh/ sounds.*

2. Demonstrate the sound of each digraph.

Point to the picture of the cherries.

Say: *The letters C and H together sound like /ch/, as in cherries.*

3. Guide the practice.

Say: *What other words can you think of that start with /ch/?*

Repeat steps 2 and 3 with the picture of the thumb and the picture of the shark.

4. Practice identifying beginning sounds.

Say: *I'll say a word and I want you to tell me which letter pattern it starts with: she. Let's try again: chin. How about thanks?*

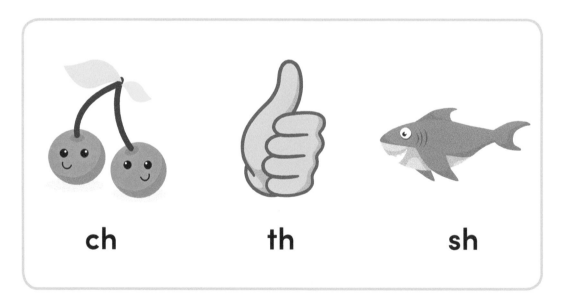

ch   th   sh

Spin a Sound

Gather coins, cereal pieces, buttons, or something similar to use as markers. Use the tip of a pencil to hold a paper clip loop to the center of the spinner. Flick the paper clip. Cover a word or picture on the grid that has the sound the paper clip lands on. See how quickly you can cover them all.

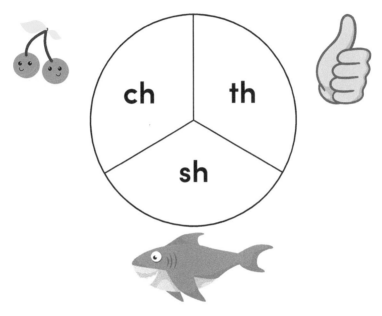

shop		chop	shin
thin	chin		
	shut		shot
with			

The -ash Word Family

1. Review.

Say: *Can you touch each dot in this word family and tell me the sound? Can you slide your finger across the arrow and blend the sounds together?*

2. Share the objective.

Say: *Today you will learn how to read words that end with /ash/.*

3. Demonstrate reading new words with -ash.

Say: *Watch how I can read more words by putting different sounds in front of /ash/.*

Touch the dot under the M in *mash* and say /m/, then slide your finger across the short arrow and say /ash/. Slide your finger across the long arrow and say "mash."

4. Guide the practice.

Say: *Now you try blending this word.*

Repeat this process with the word *cash.*

5. Practice identifying ending sounds.

Say: *I'll say a word and I want you to tell me if it ends with /ash/: stash. How about free? How about crash?*

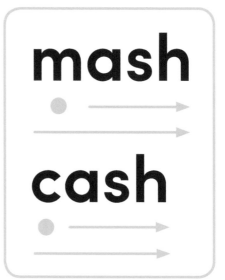

Let's Race!

Read each word around the racetrack. Can you do it again, faster? Color a star for each time you read all the way around the track.

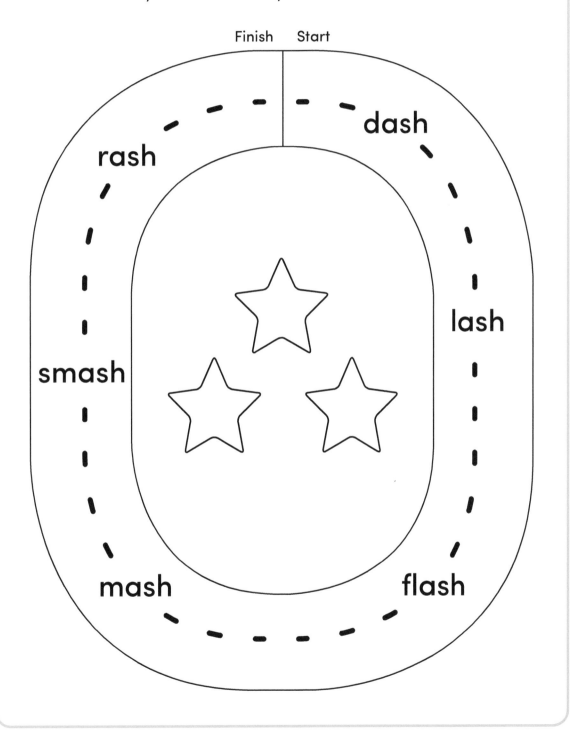

The -ush Word Family

1. Review.

Say: *Can you touch each dot in this word family and tell me the sound? Can you slide your finger across the arrow and blend the sounds together?*

2. Share the objective.

Say: *Today you will learn how to read words that end with /ush/.*

3. Demonstrate reading new words with -ush.

Say: *Watch how I can read more words by putting different sounds in front of /ush/.*

Touch the dot under the M in *mush* and say /m/, then slide your finger across the short arrow and say /ush/. Slide your finger across the long arrow and say "mush."

4. Guide the practice.

Say: *Now you try blending this word.*

Repeat this process with the word *rush.*

Search the Farm

Circle and read the words from the -ush family.

flush

hit

gush   shush   man   we

can

rush

mush

mop   hush

The -ush Word Family   **181**

The -all Word Family

1. Review.

Look back at the previous lesson and practice reading words in the -ush family.

2. Share the objective.

Say: *Today you will learn how to read words that end with /all/.*

3. Demonstrate reading new words with -all.

Say: *Watch how I can read more words by putting different sounds in front of /all/. When there are two of the same letter together, we just say the letter sound once.*

Touch the dot under the B in *ball* and say /b/, then slide your finger across the short arrow and say /all/. Slide your finger across the long arrow and say "ball."

4. Guide the practice.

Say: *Now you try blending this word.*

Repeat this process with the word *fall.*

5. Practice blending skills.

Say: *I'll say two sounds and I want you to blend them into a word: /f/ /all/, /st/ /all/, /sm/ /all/.*

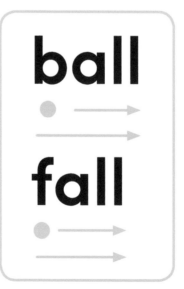

Let's Race!

Read each word around the racetrack. Can you do it again, faster? Color a star for each time you read all the way around the track.

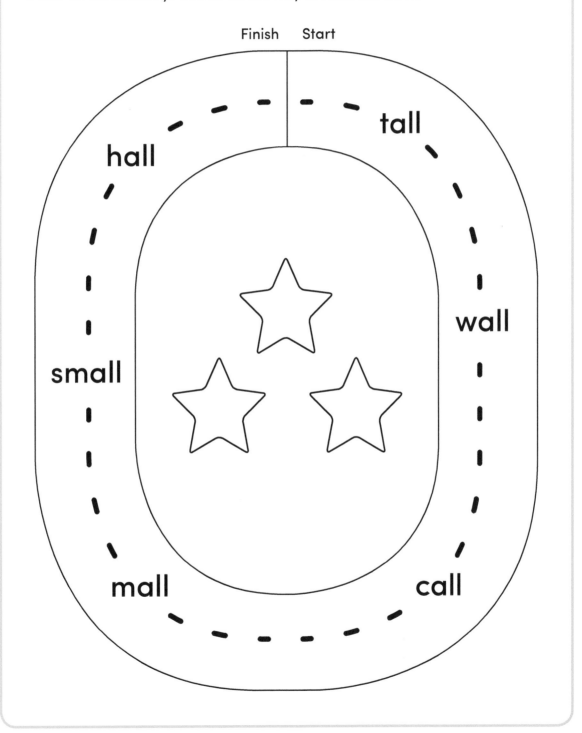

The -ell Word Family

1. Review.

Say: *When there are two of the same letter together, we just say the letter sound once. Can you touch each dot in this word family and tell me the sound? Can you slide your finger across the arrow and blend the sounds together?*

2. Share the objective.

Say: *Today you will learn how to read words that end with /ell/.*

3. Demonstrate reading new words with -ell.

Say: *Watch how I can read more words by putting different sounds in front of /ell/.*

Touch the dot under the S in *sell* and say /s/, then slide your finger across the short arrow and say /ell/. Slide your finger across the long arrow and say "sell."

4. Guide the practice.

Say: *Now you try blending this word.*

Repeat this process with the word *tell*.

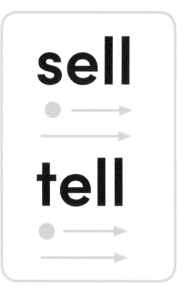

Things You Hear and See

Touch the dot under each word while you read the sentences. Color in the star when you finish each one.

I a yell.
hear
⬤　⬤　⬤　⬤

I a bell.
hear
⬤　⬤　⬤　⬤

I a shell.
see
⬤　⬤　⬤　⬤

I a well.
see
⬤　⬤　⬤　⬤

The -ill Word Family

1. Review.

Say: *Remember that when there are two of the same letter together, we just say the letter sound once. Can you touch each dot in this word family and tell me the sound? Can you slide your finger across the arrow and blend the sounds together?*

2. Share the objective.

Say: *Today you will learn how to read words that end with /ill/.*

3. Demonstrate reading new words with -ill.

Say: *Watch how I can read more words by putting different sounds in front of /ill/.*

Touch the dot under the B in *bill* and say /b/, then slide your finger across the short arrow and say /ill/. Slide your finger across the long arrow and say "bill."

4. Guide the practice.

Say: *Now you try blending this word.*

Repeat this process with the word *fill*.

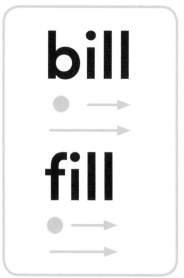

Use the Clues

Read each clue. Circle the picture that shows what the clue is talking about.

I will fill it.

●   ●   ●   ●

I will spill it.

●   ●   ●   ●

I will grill it.

●   ●   ●   ●

I will chill it.

●   ●   ●   ●

Review the Word Families -all, -ell, and -ill

1. Share the objective.

Say: *Today we'll practice the -all, -ell, and -ill word families.*

2. Demonstrate reading word families.

Point to the letters A-L-L.

Say: *This says /all/ like at the end of "ball."*

3. Guide the practice.

Say: *What other words can you think of that end with -all?*

Repeat steps two and three with the letters E-L-L and I-L-L.

4. Practice listening for ending sounds.

Say: *I'll say a word and you tell me which pattern you hear at the end: tall, will, sell.*

all   **ell**   **ill**

Spin and Go

Choose something to mark your place, like a coin or a piece of cereal, and put it on the start arrow. Use the tip of a pencil to hold a paper clip loop to the center of the spinner. Flick the paper clip. Move forward to the next word that matches the word family on the spinner and read it. How fast can you get to the end of the path?

call

tell

will

small

bell

pill

mall

shell

wall

drill

tall

spill

smell

The /ck/ Sound

1. Share the objective.

Say: *Today you will learn how to listen for words with the /ck/ sound.*

2. Demonstrate the sound of the digraph.

Say: *The letters C and K are special because they work together to make one sound. That sound is /ck/, like at the end of sock. We use the C-K pattern only in the middle or at the end of words, not at the beginning.*

Listen for the /ck/ at the end of these words.

Point to each picture and read the words.

3. Guide the practice.

Say: *Can you circle the C-K at the end of each of these words?*

4. Practice blending skills.

Say: *I'll say three sounds and I want you to put them together to make a word: /kn/ /o/ /ck/, /tr/ /i/ /ck/, /bl/ /o/ /ck/.*

ck

rock

duck

neck

One Stuck Duck

Color the boxes with a picture that ends with a /ck/ sound to make a path for the duck to get to the pond.

Reading Words with the /ck/ Sound

1. Review.

Look back at the previous lesson and practice naming the pictures with the ck digraph.

2. Share the objective.

Say: *Today you will learn how to read words that have the sound /ck/.*

3. Demonstrate reading words with /ck/.

Say: *Listen to how I say the C and K together as one sound when I read these words.*

Touch the dots while you say each sound in the word *luck*. Then slide your finger across the arrow and say the whole word. Repeat with the word *pack*.

4. Guide the practice.

Say: *Can you read the sounds and then the whole word for the last two examples?*

Which Is Right?

Read each sentence. Circle the word that belongs in the blank to match the picture.

I am _____.

kick   **sick**

I am _____.

stuck   **sock**

I am _____.

Jack   **pick**

I am _____.

neck   **back**

The -ack Word Family

1. Review.

Say: *Can you touch each dot in this word family and tell me the sound? Can you slide your finger across the arrow and blend the sounds together?*

2. Share the objective.

Say: *Today you will learn how to read words that end with /ack/.*

3. Demonstrate reading new words with -ack.

Say: *Watch how I can read more words by putting different sounds in front of /ack/.*

Touch the dot under the T in *tack* and say /t/, then slide your finger across the short arrow and say /ack/. Slide your finger across the long arrow and say "tack."

4. Guide the practice.

Say: *Now you try blending this word.*

Repeat this process with the word *back.*

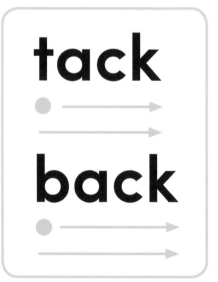

Read and Match

Read each sentence. Draw a line to connect each sentence to the matching picture.

You have a snack.

You have a pack.

You have a sack.

You have a tack.

You have a stack.

The -ick Word Family

1. Review.

Say: *Can you touch each dot in this word family and tell me the sound? Can you slide your finger across the arrow and blend the sounds together?*

2. Share the objective.

Say: *Today you will learn how to read words that end with /ick/.*

3. Demonstrate reading new words with -ick.

Say: *Watch how I can read more words by putting different sounds in front of /ick/.*

Touch the dot under the P in *pick* and say /p/, then slide your finger across the short arrow and say /ick/. Slide your finger across the long arrow and say "pick."

4. Guide the practice.

Say: *Now you try blending this word.*

Repeat this process with the word *kick.*

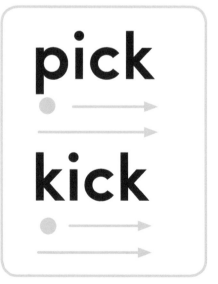

Connect to the Center

Draw a line from each word or picture that ends with -ick to the letters in the center.

click

trick

ick

brick

spin

The -ock Word Family

1. Review.

Say: *Can you touch each dot in this word family and tell me the sound? Can you slide your finger across the arrow and blend the sounds together?*

2. Share the objective.

Say: *Today you will learn how to read words that end with /ock/.*

3. Demonstrate reading new words with -ock.

Say: *Watch how I can read more words by putting different sounds in front of /ock/.*

Touch the dot under the L in *lock* and say /l/, then slide your finger across the short arrow and say /ock/. Slide your finger across the long arrow and say "lock."

4. Guide the practice.

Say: *Now you try blending this word.*

Repeat this process with the word *rock*.

5. Practice rhyming skills.

Say: *Can you think of another word that rhymes with lock and rock?*

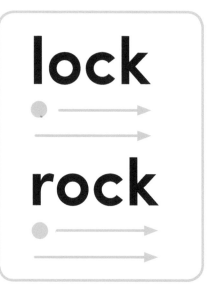

A Silly Shopping Trip

Touch the dot under each word while you read the sentences. Color in the star when you finish each one.

We get a block.

   •   •   •   •

We get a clock.

   •   •   •   •

We get a sock.

   •   •   •   •

We get a lock.

   •   •   •   •

Sight Word *this*

1. Share the objective.

Say: *Today you will learn the word* this.

2. Demonstrate reading the new word.

Point to the two versions of the word *this* and say: *Both of these words say "this." One starts with a big T and the other starts with a small T. Watch how I read it in a sentence.*

Touch the dot under each word as you read the first sentence.

3. Guide the practice.

Say: *Now you try touching the dots and reading each sentence.*

This   This is fun.
              •   •   •

this   This is big.
              •   •   •

Fill in a Face

Read each sentence. If it matches the picture, color the happy face. If it does not match the picture, color the sad face.

This is a cat.

This is a box.

This is a pan.

This is a hen.

This is a cub.

This is a bed.

Sight Word *for*

1. Review.

Look back at the previous lesson and practice reading the word *this*.

2. Share the objective.

Say: *Today you will learn the word* for.

3. Demonstrate reading the new word.

Point to the two versions of the word *for* and say: *Both of these words say "for." One starts with a big F and the other starts with a small F. Watch how I read it in a sentence.*

Touch the dot under each word as you read the first sentence.

4. Guide the practice.

Say: *Now you try touching the dots and reading each sentence.*

| For | This is for Mom. |

| for | This is for Ben. |

Sight Word Squawk

Use the code to color the picture. Choose any color for areas that do not have a word.

for

this

was

in

RESOURCES

For Teaching Beginner Readers

Literacy and Young Children: Research-Based Practices (Solving Problems in the Teaching of Literacy) by Diane M. Barone (Editor) and Lesley Mandel Morrow (Editor): This book presents research-based approaches for meeting children at their level of literacy knowledge and guiding them to more complex concepts.

Beyond Baby Talk by Kenn Apel and Julie Masterson: Learn about a child's language and literacy development, including ideas to boost reading, spelling, and writing abilities in this book.

Starting Out Right: A Guide to Promoting Children's Reading Success by M. Susan Burns (Editor), Peg Griffin (Editor), and Catherine E. Snow (Editor) and the National Research Council: This book aims to help parents and caregivers prepare children for literacy instruction by the time they get to school.

By Different Paths to Common Outcomes by Marie M. Clay: Aimed at teachers, this text describes ways to observe and build on what children already know about literacy so that every child, regardless of level, can make progress.

Early Childhood Literacy: The National Early Literacy Panel and Beyond by Timothy Shanahan (Editor) and Christopher J. Lonigan (Editor): Based on the ideas in the National Early Literacy Panel Report, this book recommends best practices in early literacy instruction.

Literacy Beginnings: A Prekindergarten Handbook by Gay Su Pinnell and Irene Fountas: The authors of this book dig into the relationship between language and play, and how young children learn about the world.

Starting Strong: Evidence-Based Early Literacy Practices by Katrin Blamey and Katherine Beauchat: This book describes literacy skills that young children need and matches the skills with information from research and ideas instruction.

Starfall, www.starfall.com: This website is full of engaging activities that let children practice letter sounds and other literacy skills on the computer.

The Measured Mom, www.themeasuredmom.com: Find ideas on this website for practicing letters, sight words, phonics patterns, and more.

This Reading Mama, www.thisreadingmama.com: This site has a great collection of printable reading games and ideas to reinforce learning letters and words.

For the Next Level of Instruction

Making Words—First Grade: 100 Hands-On Lessons for Phonemic Awareness, Phonics and Spelling by Patricia M. Cunningham and Dorothy P. Hall: The activities in this book offer more in-depth study of phonics patterns that help children spell and read.

Phonics They Use: Words for Reading and Writing by Patricia M. Cunningham: This book focuses on reading fluency, rhyme-based decoding, and how children use phonics to help them read and write.

The Book Whisperer: Awakening the Inner Reader in Every Child by Donalyn Miller: This book takes a step outside of skill instruction and focuses on how to encourage a love of reading in children.

Reading in the Wild: The Book Whisperer's Keys to Cultivating Lifelong Reading Habits by Donalyn Miller and Susan Kelley: Building on *The Book Whisperer*, this texts digs into how to encourage lifelong reading.

Reading Essentials: The Specifics You Need to Teach Reading Well by Regie Routman: This is an indispensable guide for reading teachers. It dives deep into using the releasing-support method in the reading classroom.

Making Sense of Phonics, The First Edition: The Hows and Whys by Isabel L. Beck: Learn more ways to build children's reading skills with more advanced phonics in this book.

The Ordinary Parent's Guide to Teaching Reading by Jessie Wise and Sara Buffington: Designed for parents, this book presents lessons for guiding children to more complex phonics skills.

ReadWriteThink, www.readwritethink.org: This website has a great collection of lessons and activities to reinforce more complex phonics skills.

Oxford Owl, www.oxfordowl.co.uk: This website has a great collection of ebooks for young readers, some with activities. A free account is required to use the site.

ABCya!, www.abcya.com: Many fun reading games can be found on this website, progressing all the way up to fifth-grade skills. The site is free to use on a PC, but does show ads on the side.

ABOUT THE AUTHOR

Hannah Braun is a curriculum author specializing in learning materials for primary-grade students. Her passion for teaching young learners comes through in her engaging activities. Hannah holds a bachelor's degree in elementary education and a master's degree in early childhood education. She refined her teaching expertise through eight years in an elementary school classroom working with diverse learners. Raising two children of her own has also contributed to Hannah's understanding of child development and learning. Additionally, Hannah authors the blog *The Classroom Key* (TheClassroomKey.com), where she shares ideas and best practices for teaching. In her free time, Hannah enjoys paper crafting and fitness classes. Follow her on Facebook or Instagram, both @TheClassroomKey.

CPSIA information can be obtained
at www.ICGtesting.com
Printed in the USA
LVHW051504201118
597736LV00007B/159/P

9 781939 754523